FIELD GUIDE

TO THE

MAMMALS

OF THE

INDIAN SUBCONTINENT

Where to Watch Mammals in India, Nepal, Bhutan, Bangladesh,
Sri Lanka and Pakistan

K K GURUNG

and

RAJ SINGH

Colour plates by Zillah Richards and black and white plates
and line drawings by K K Gurung

ACADEMIC PRESS
Harcourt Brace & Company, Publishers
SAN DIEGO   LONDON   BOSTON
NEW YORK   SYDNEY   TOKYO   TORONTO

AP Natural World is published by
ACADEMIC PRESS
525B Street, Suite 1900, San Diego,
California 92101–4495, USA
http://www.apnet.com

ACADEMIC PRESS LIMITED
24–28 Oval Road
LONDON NW1 7DX
http://www.hbuk.co.uk/ap/

First published by Indian Experience, Oxford. 1996

Published separately in India, Nepal, Bangladesh, Sri Lanka, and Pakistan

A catalogue record for this book is available from the British Library

ISBN 0–12–309350–3

Typeset by Wyvern 21 Ltd, Bristol
Printed in Great Britain by WBC, Bridgend, Mid Glamorgan

98 99 00 01 02 WBC 9 8 7 6 5 4 3 2 1

For
Deborah, James and Nicholas Gurung
and
Diane and Arjun Singh

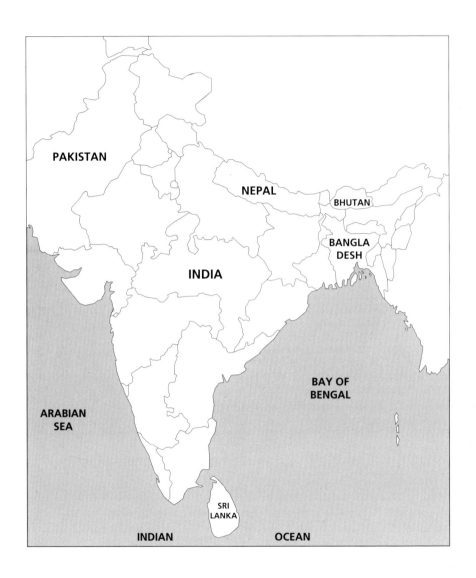

CONTENTS

COLOUR PLATES

BLACK AND WHITE PLATES: Animal Tracks

PREFACE

The Indian subcontinent occupies the southern edge of Asia and consists of India, Nepal, Bhutan, Bangladesh, Sri Lanka and Pakistan. Mountains, notably the Hindu Kush and Himalaya ranges that rise up to 8848 metres on Everest, bound the upper, northern, half of this diamond-shaped area. The southern parts jut into the Indian Ocean. Great rivers like the Indus, Ganges and Brahmaputra water the land.

Within its boundaries there are a fantastic variety of habitats, ranging from the tropical to the arctic, including desert, scrub, mangrove and forest. The subcontinent is also one of the most heavily populated regions on earth, with over 1.2 billion people.

Despite its human population, the subcontinent harbours a great diversity of mammals. Some species are large and spectacular, like the Tiger, Indian Elephant and Indian Rhinoceros. Others, like the Ratel, Red Panda and Spotted Linsang, are less well known, even amongst the locals.

During the last two decades, we have travelled extensively in the subcontinent and we have felt frustrated by the lack of a suitable field guide to the mammals and the best mammal watching areas. We hope that this book fulfils that need.

We have given descriptions of each of the 100 plus species that can be recognised in the field, including identification, habitat, range, behaviour, diet, breeding, status, and similar species. Each species included in the book has been illustrated in colour. And there are black and white plates of the tracks of the more prominent mammals. This section should be particularly useful, as mammals of the Indian subcontinent are generally shy and not easy to see. It is possible to identify a number of species by their distinctive tracks.

Of the hundreds of protected areas, large and small, we decided to include only the very finest. With great difficulty we narrowed down our list to 23 national parks and national park groups. Together they include most of the habitat types and mammal fauna of the subcontinent. Some are remote with limited tourist infrastructure, like Namdapha and Sunderbans. Others, like Chitwan and Corbett, are easily accessible and with good facilities. We have included a mammal list and map for each national park.

We hope that this book will help popularise the mammals of the Indian subcontinent and add to the enjoyment and understanding of this fascinating animal group.

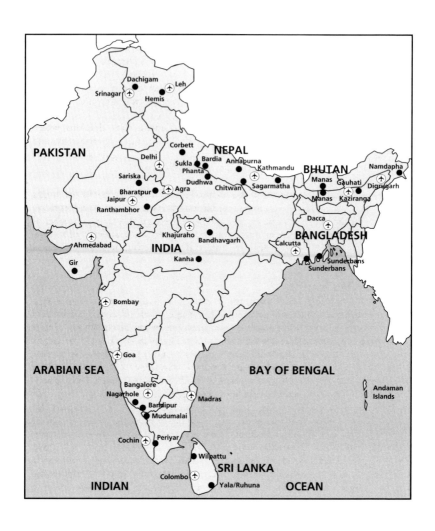

INTRODUCTION

WHAT ARE MAMMALS?

Mammals are vertebrates or animals with backbones, as are reptiles, birds, fish and amphibians. They are also endothermic or "warm-blooded"; they maintain a relatively constant body temperature, independent of the temperature of their surroundings, as do birds. (Reptiles and amphibians are exothermic or "cold-blooded", their body temperatures change relative to the temperature of their surroundings.) However, the most characteristic features of mammals that distinguish them from all other groups of animals are the presence of body hair and mammary or milk glands in females.

The skin of mammals is covered in hair. Exceptions include whales and dolphins, which are hairless as adults but have some hair during their embryonic development, and elephants and rhinoceroses, which have reduced hair The pangolin's scales, the porcupine's quills and the rhinoceros's horn, are all modified hair.

Female mammals nourish their young with milk produced from highly specialised organs called mammary or milk glands. Mammals give birth to their young, except the primitive mammals (the Prototheria) who, like reptiles and birds, lay eggs. There are a number of other less obvious unique features of mammals (eg the lower jaw is made up of a single bone, the dentary, and they have a distinctive skeletal pattern), but these are of interest only to the specialist.

MAMMAL DIVERSITY

Worldwide, some 4,500 species of mammals are known to us today, of which roughly a tenth occur within the Indian subcontinent. They range in size from tiny shrews and pipistrelle bats, which weigh a few grammes and measure a few centimetres, to elephants that stand over 3 metres at the shoulder and can weigh over 4 tonnes. The largest mammal, the Blue Whale, is nearly 30 metres in length and weighs up to 150 tonnes. Mammals are remarkably diverse in form and structure. Bats, which fly like birds, and are mainly denizens of the dark, possess a sophisticated echolocation system for navigation. Whales, dolphins and porpoises, like fish, have colonized the seas. Monkeys and squirrels are excellent tree climbers and flying squirrels have adapted to use the parachute-like membranes between their limbs to glide long distances from tree to tree. The larger terrestrial mammals, like the Tiger, bears and deer live on the ground, where food, water and shelter are available. Many smaller mammals, like foxes and otters, shelter in burrows made in the ground. Moles lead a largely subterranean existence and are almost totally blind. Through their remarkable adaptations, mammals inhabit every conceivable habitat: from deserts to the arctic conditions on the Himalayan slopes, from mangrove swamps to dense forests, from small lakes to the mighty Ganges river, and even urban areas close to man.

MAIN GEOGRAPHICAL REGIONS OF THE SUBCONTINENT

The Indian subcontinent (consisting of India, Nepal, Bhutan, Bangladesh, Sri Lanka and Pakistan) is the shape of a huge diamond covering an area of nearly 4.5 million sq km, roughly half the size of the USA, and lies at the southern edge of Asia. It is bound by Iran and Afghanistan to the west, Tibet and China to the north, Myanmar (Burma) to the east, and the Bay of Bengal and the Arabian Sea to the South. The island of Sri Lanka lies off the southern tip of India in the Indian Ocean. Within the subcontinent there are

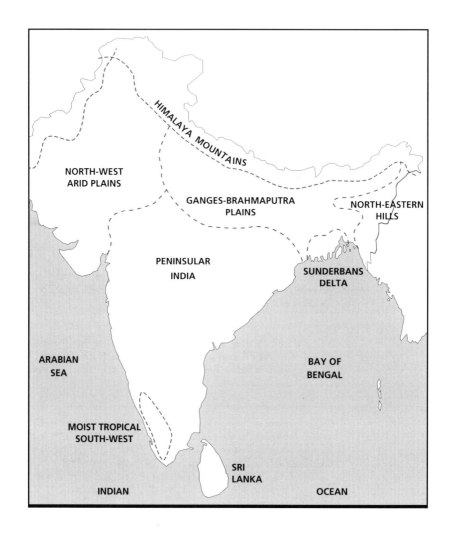

HIMALAYA MOUNTAINS

NORTH-WEST
ARID PLAINS

GANGES-BRAHMAPUTRA
PLAINS

NORTH-EASTERN
HILLS

PENINSULAR
INDIA

SUNDERBANS
DELTA

ARABIAN
SEA

BAY OF
BENGAL

MOIST TROPICAL
SOUTH-WEST

SRI
LANKA

INDIAN

OCEAN

a number of distinct geographical regions which have been described below. For each geographical region we have given a list of mammals that are representative of that region (but may also be found in other regions).

Himalaya Mountains
Along the northern frontier of the subcontinent, including parts of Northern Pakistan, India, Nepal and Bhutan, lies the great arc of the Himalaya, the highest range of mountains in the world, culminating in Mount Everest at 8,848 metres. Many Palaearctic species are found here, like the Brown Bear, Red Deer, Stoat, Bharal, Snow Leopard and Lesser Panda. The Himalaya is roughly 2,000 km long, so Central Asian species are represented in the Western Himalaya and Indo-Chinese species in the Eastern Himalaya.

Ganges-Brahmaputra Plains
The alluvial plains of the Ganges and the Brahmaputra river basins lie to the south of the Himalaya. This region also includes the Himalayan foothills, the 'dun' valleys and the moist 'terai' and 'duar' plains. Rhesus Macaque, Pygmy Hog, Hispid Hare, Indian Rhinoceros, Tiger, Golden Leaf Monkey and Swamp Deer are found here.

Sunderbans Delta
The low lying Sunderbans delta, the largest in the world, formed by the Ganges, Brahmaputra and Meghna rivers in India and Bangladesh, is subject to heavy sedimentation from the rivers, especially during the monsoon floods, and periodic inundations by the Bay of Bengal. Mammals here have adapted to a semi-aquatic existence, including the Tiger, Wild Boar and Spotted Deer.

North-Eastern Hills
The hills of North-Eastern India and Eastern Bangladesh, are covered in tropical rainforests. Several Malayan species are found here, including the Hoolock Gibbon, Asiatic Golden Cat, Clouded Leopard and Binturong.

North-West Arid Plains
The arid and semi-arid belt of land covering the North-Western Indian states of Punjab, Haryana, Rajasthan and Gujarat, and Pakistan further to the west, holds several species from Arabia and the adjoining areas including the Asiatic Lion, Asiatic Wild Ass, Indian Gazelle and Wild Cat.

Peninsular India
Jutting into the Indian Ocean, south of the Ganges-Brahmaputra plains, is the triangular southern landmass of India, also known as the Peninsula or the Deccan. Much of it is a plateau and along its eastern and the western coasts run the Eastern and the Western Ghats which still harbour large forested areas. Because of its remoteness and distance from other biogeographical regions, the Peninsula may be regarded as largely Indian, with mammals such as the Bonnet Macaque, Nilgai, Rusty-spotted Cat and Blackbuck.

Moist Tropical South-West
Distinct from the Peninsula, on India's South-West corner, are the moist tropical hill forests of Kerala, Karnataka and Tamilnadu, characterised by evergreen 'shola' forests which cover the southern one-third of the Western Ghats. This area shares some of the characteristics of the North-Eastern Hill forests. Mammals include the Liontail Macaque, Nilgiri Tahr and Nilgiri Langur.

Sri Lanka

Separated from the southern tip of India by the narrow Palk Strait is the island of Sri Lanka which shares many Peninsular species, although it does have a few endemic mammals, like the Toque Macaque and the Purple-faced Monkey. In the absence of the Tiger, which colonized southern India after Sri Lanka had broken away from the landmass and formed an island, the Leopard is the dominant predator and is often seen during the day.

MAMMALS UNIQUE TO THE INDIAN SUBCONTINENT

The Indian subcontinent shares many mammal species that belong, zoogeographically, to regions to its east, west and north. There are a number of species, however, that are unique to the subcontinent, including the following:

Bonnet Macaque	Macaca radiata
Liontail Macaque	Macaca silenus
Golden Leaf Monkey	Presbytis geei
Nilgiri Langur	Presbytis johnii
Sloth Bear	Melursus ursinus
Ganges Dolphin	Platanista gangetica
Indian Rhinoceros	Rhinoceros unicornis
Pygmy Hog	Sus salvanius
Chital	Cervus axis
Swamp Deer	Cervus duvauceli
Nilgai	Boselaphus tragocamelus
Four-horned Antelope	Tetracerus quadricornis
Blackbuck	Antilope cervicapra
Nilgiri Tahr	Hemitragus hylocrius
Hispid Hare	Caprolagus hispidus

HOW TO USE THIS BOOK

This book is a field guide to the larger, more distinctive mammals of the Indian subcontinent. Only those species that can be identified in their natural habitat with reasonable success have been included. We have not included smaller species like rats, mice, shrews and bats, that are difficult or impossible to identify without a close examination of a specimen in hand. Marine mammals have also been excluded.

The book has two sections: the first deals with the identification of mammal species and the second with the main national parks for mammal watching.

It should be stressed at the outset that, with a few exceptions, we still know relatively little about the mammals of the Indian subcontinent. Hence there is a dearth of information about mammal behaviour, ecology, breeding, etc for most species. We have tried to include all the material that will assist you in identifying mammals in the field. Technical information has been kept to a minimum. You are advised to resort to the process of elimination if you spot a species but are unsure of its identity.

We have used the following format in describing each mammal species.

Common names
The common English name of the species is given in block capitals (additional names are in brackets). We have generally followed the names adopted by G B Corbet and J E Hill in 'A World List of Mammalian Species'. Additional names, if used, have been taken largely from S H Prater's 'The Book of Indian Animals'. Elsewhere in the text the common names always begin with a capital letter, eg Golden Leaf Monkey, or Rusty-spotted Cat.

Scientific or Latin names
The scientific name consists of two parts: the Genus, which starts with a capital letter, and the species, which starts with a small letter. For example, Panthera (genus) tigris (species). While a species may be known by many names in different languages, or even within the same language, it is normally given one scientific name that is generally acceptable. However, as our understanding of mammals increases, scientific names may also be revised from time to time, as new light is shed on their classification. This, for example, has already happened with many species of Felids or cats, but we have chosen to keep the older, more familiar names. The scientific names used are mainly from the book by G B Corbet and J E Hill.

Identification
As all the mammals featured in this book have been illustrated in colour, only a brief description of the species is given. Sizes are approximate and do not necessarily include minimum and maximum measurements. Colours vary considerably, depending upon the habitat, the time of year, the age and the sex of the animal, lighting conditions and individual variation within a population. A tiger at 25 metres in broad daylight may appear golden yellow, while in the evening at 100 metres, it looks dark red. Colour illustrations depict typical adult males, unless otherwise stated in the colour plates.

Habitat
Only the major habitats used by a species are mentioned. However, mammals are very adaptable creatures and may occasionally occur in habitats not described here.

Range
We have tried to mention only the general distribution of the species within the Indian subcontinent. Many of the species occur outside our boundaries as well, but no mention of that has been made. The species under discussion may not be found throughout the indicated range, but only where suitable habitats exist. Some species are fairly widespread in their range, like the Rhesus Macaque. Others are highly localised, like the Red Deer, Swamp Deer and the Golden Leaf Monkey, due to their more specialised habitat requirements. The range is a useful tool in identification as it helps to eliminate certain species when a sighting is inconclusive.

Behaviour
Brief points about the ecology and behaviour of the mammals have been given. In most cases our understanding of mammal behaviour and ecology is limited and incomplete.

Diet
For the sake of brevity, a general list of the types of foods preferred by each species has been given. For example, 'small mammals' rather than the specific species eaten. It is

quite possible that the species in question will feed upon other food types as well.

Breeding
This gives information about gestation periods, numbers born in a litter, longevity, etc. This information is largely obtained by scientists from observing captive animals. Longevity in the wild will most likely be shorter than in captivity.

Status
The status relates to the Indian subcontinent only. The following status keys have been used:

Endangered	threatened with extinction
Vulnerable	in danger, but no threat of extinction yet
Insufficiently known	may be endangered or vulnerable; could also be common or abundant
Uncommon	rare, very difficult to see
Common	relatively easy to see
Abundant	assured sighting

It should be noted that endangered and vulnerable species may be locally common, eg the Indian Rhinoceros in Kaziranga and Chitwan, Golden Leaf Monkey in Manas, and Lion in Gir.

Similar species
Only those species that occur within the Indian subcontinent and that might be confused in the field have been included. Similar species are listed even if they occur in geographically isolated habitats. This should help minimise errors in identification. If a similar species occurs in the subcontinent but is not featured in this book then we have specified its range. Some of the similar species mentioned may, on closer examination, be quite different in appearance (size, colour, etc). In the field, however, one often only gets a fleeting glimpse of a species, especially those that are rare, solitary and elusive, which makes the task of positive identification difficult. Looking up the illustrations and the text on the similar species can help you to eliminate unlikely species.

MAPS
All the maps are approximate and should only be used as rough guides. The national and international boundaries have no political significance. The maps of the national parks are also approximate, with only a few features shown, and they are not intended for use as road maps or to locate the lodges and hotels in the area. We would like to have featured more landmarks in and around the national parks, but this has not been possible due to a lack of space or information.

MAMMAL CONSERVATION
Almost all the national parks in the Indian subcontinent that harbour sizeable mammal populations today were the hunting preserves of the former rulers of the many princely states and kingdoms in India, Pakistan, Bangladesh, and Sri Lanka, and of the present day kings in Nepal and Bhutan. Large chunks of forests were given strict protection, if only

to ensure that they provided sustainable yields for the annual shoots. Up until the early 20th century, extensive forests remained, but excessive hunting was already taking its toll, particularly on the big game. The Indian Rhinoceros in Kaziranga and the Lion in Gir were fast heading towards extinction and were only brought back from the very brink by strict protection. After the British rule in the Indian subcontinent ended in the late 1940s, many of the former hunting preserves came under the jurisdiction of the national and state governments. However, it was only in the 1970s that the conservation movement gathered real momentum, with the launch in India of Project Tiger in 1973, under which special Tiger Reserves were designated for the protection of the Tiger whose numbers had fallen to fewer than 2,000. Today, there are a few hundred protected areas, large and small, in the subcontinent, specially set aside for the conservation of mammals and other wildlife. But these protected areas are often 'islands' within vast seas of human habitation and cultivation. With a human population of 1.2 billion which is still growing, the future of the subcontinent's wildlife and wilderness areas remains extremely uncertain. Deforestation and hunting still remain the biggest threats to their long term survival. (Hereafter, the term national park or park is used to mean any protected area).

OBSERVING MAMMALS

Although the subcontinent has a rich and diversified mammal fauna, including some large and conspicuous species, it is not always easy to spot and study. Mammals are generally shy and silent and many species are nocturnal, especially in areas where human disturbance is high. Birds, on the other hand, are usually less shy, far more vocal and are largely active by day (also, there are 1,250 species of birds compared to some 450 species of mammals in the subcontinent). Mammals make very good use of their surroundings (forest, grass, rocks, etc) to conceal themselves. It is possible to not spot a rhino, elephant or tiger at a distance of only 25 metres in the jungle! In contrast to the smaller mammals like rats, mice, shrews and bats, which often occur in vast numbers, most of the larger mammals occur in low densities, thus adding to the difficulty of observing them. Mammals are remarkably adaptable and some live in close proximity to man (eg certain species of rats and mice, jackals, palm civets, palm-squirrels, etc). Most large mammals, however, prefer to live away from human habitation, in forests and wilderness areas that are relatively free from disturbance. Perhaps we should also stress that mammal watching in the Indian subcontinent is very different from that in the Eastern or Southern African bush. Herbivores living on the open African plains are generally gregarious, often forming huge assemblies of up to several hundred animals. They are not particularly shy and may be observed at close quarters from a vehicle. The larger predators, like the African Lion, Wild Dog and Spotted Hyaena, live and hunt in family groups, making for easier observation. In contrast, the forests of the subcontinent are dense with poor visibility for much of the year, and the mammals that live in such habitats are usually retiring and are often solitary or live in small groups. The larger predators, like the Tiger and the Leopard, mainly live and hunt alone. Many of the subcontinent's national parks are either in the hills or in remote areas unsuitable for human habitation, like the Sunderbans mangrove swamps. (The low-lying fertile and more accessible areas have long since been cleared for farming and human settlement). Observing mammals in broken and hilly terrain is far more difficult, due to the restricted visibility and access and the fact that such habitats generally support a smaller mammal biomass than the richer grasslands of the plains. In Chitwan National Park, Nepal, which has both kinds of habitat, the grasslands support far more herbivores than the hill forests. However, these 'adverse' conditions, make the thrill of mammal watching in the subcontinent far more exciting. A safari on elephant back, through 6 metre tall 'elephant grass', with the possibility of a chance encounter with a Tiger, Sloth Bear or Indian

Rhinoceros, can be an exhilarating and rewarding experience.

Most mammals have excellent senses of sight, hearing and smell, and the human visitor needs to be as inconspicuous, quiet and odourless as possible. For successful mammal watching you will need to be appropriately dressed. In the jungle, casual clothes in khaki, olive green or camouflage, are recommended to help you to blend in and be less conspicuous. Wear comfortable shoes, and a floppy hat will be necessary as a shield from the sun. In mountain areas, trekking boots and dark sunglasses are essential. Do not smoke or wear a scent, and, if feasible, never approach mammals if the wind or breeze, however gentle, is blowing from you towards them. Do not make any noise (talk in whispers, if you have to), and take care to walk as silently as possible. Thankfully, many mammals will allow you to approach relatively close to them on elephant back or from boats or motor vehicles. It is best to keep the engine running, as this muffles your noise and enables you to get away quickly if the mammal in question decides to see you off.

Unlike birdwatching, which can produce a list of 100 species in a good day in some parks, eg Chitwan and Corbett, it is important to set aside a reasonable length of time to seek out the mammals, especially the more elusive ones. We recommend 4-5 days for each park, although this may not always be feasible because of a lack of time. Chance also plays a major role. Forest guards have been known to spend months or years in a park without seeing a Tiger or Leopard, while visitors may see them on their first outing. The time of year can also make a big difference to successful mammal watching. Generally speaking, the spring and the early summer are the best times for visiting national parks. At that time the vegetation is less dense, so it is easier to spot mammals, and the general shortage of water attracts them to waterholes. However, in most non-Himalayan national parks, temperatures in the summer can soar to 40 degrees C. If you prefer milder temperatures then travel during the cooler months of October through March, which also coincides with the general tourist season. Here is a rough guide to the seasons, mammal sightings and clothing:

October-January	Cool to cold; good sightings; may be misty in the early mornings; take warm clothing.
February-May	Warm to hot; excellent sightings; beware of the heat; take cool cotton clothing.
June-September	Monsoon; generally poor sightings; frequent heavy rains; take rain-proof clothing; many parks are inaccessible or closed.

MAMMAL WATCHER'S TOOL-KIT

It is essential to carry a pair of 8x or 10x magnification binoculars. Those equipped with protective rubber covers are preferable to metal binoculars which tend to glint in the sun. Take a small note book, pencil, pencil-sharpener and eraser, for taking relevant notes. The more serious mammal-watchers will need a 3 metre tape to measure things of interest, such as the size of caves, droppings, antlers, tracks, claw marks, etc. Notes should include the date, time of day, name of place, type of habitat, and the details of any observations made. Include all the key sights, sounds and smells of the subject of observation. Where possible, draw sketches, even very rough ones, especially if it is not possible to photograph your subject. Tracks are best drawn on the spot (they are notoriously difficult to get good photographs of). While taking pictures of tracks, use a familiar object such as a pencil or binoculars as a size reference. The casting of tracks in plaster of Paris is both time consuming and cumbersome and tracks found in mediums such as fine sand or soft snow, which are excellent for identification purposes, are extremely difficult to make castings of. On long outings it is essential to take enough drinking water (sturdy water bottles are usually available from camping shops or army surplus stores). Also take adequate supplies of insect repellent (the milder the smell the better) to discourage mosquitoes and other biting insects which can be a nuisance.

ACKNOWLEDGMENTS

The work on this book began several years ago, when the initial drafts of this manuscript were written. It has subsequently been revised to try and bring it up to date. The book draws from the scholarship of numerous naturalists who have studied and written about the mammals of the Indian subcontinent and the adjoining areas. A selection of their works is to be seen in the section on Further Reading in the book. In alphabetical order, we list the main authors whose publications we have constantly referred to: G B Corbet and J E Hill, B Lekagul and J McNeely, D Macdonald, R M Nowak, W W A Phillips, S H Prater, and T J Roberts. Over the past 20 years we have also benefited from the wisdom and knowledge of scientists, amateur naturalists, national park wardens, 'shikaris' (game trackers), 'mahouts' or 'phanits' (elephant keepers) and local people living in or near the park's edge, who have passed on information by word-of-mouth rather than through print. We have also consulted several excellent IUCN publications, management plans of several national parks, published and unpublished manuscripts, and numerous issues of the Journal of the Bombay Natural History Society, Hornbill, Sanctuary Magazine and Tiger Paper. We sincerely acknowledge our indebtedness to them all. However, we take responsibility for any errors in this book.

K K Gurung wishes to thank the management and staff at the British Museum (Natural History), London, for allowing him the use of their excellent library and for access to the mammal specimens in their collection. During his many years in Chitwan, he received encouragement and support from a number of friends, colleagues and associates, notably, Dr Charles and Margaret McDougal, Jim and Belinda Edwards, Dhan Bahadur Tamang, naturalists and nature guides. The Scientific Exploration Society kindly provided additional literature on Namdapha.

A very special thanks to Rahul Brijnath who read through the entire draft and spent many hours editing certain sections of the book. Alison Morris read the final draft and corrected the English. Raj Singh wishes to specially thank the following for their help in furnishing and collecting information on national parks of India: Bholu Khan, V D Sharma, R G Soni, Fateh Singh Rathore, Sri Ram, Anoop Wadhwa, Arun Deo, Akbar Hussain, Raghu Rao, Vinod Goswami, V Nair, S Mohan, E Flanders, Shanta Menon, Shama, Shish Ram and S Negi.

MAMMAL SPECIES

1. SLOW LORIS *(Plate 1)*
Nycticebus coucang

Identification: Head and body 26-40 cm. Tail very short (5 cm),
hidden in the fur. Fur dense. A stocky loris with a round head and large round eyes with
dark or brown eye patches. Colour variable, generally rust, yellow or grey, with lighter
head and shoulders. Distinctive dark brown dorsal stripe to the middle of crown.
Habitat: Tropical rain forests.
Range: NE India and Bangladesh.
Behaviour: Nocturnal. Secretive. Largely arboreal. Territorial, scent marking with urine.
Slow and deliberate movement. Numbers usually seen, 1-3 animals. Known to also eat
and drink hanging upside down from a branch. Ambushes prey.
Diet: Shoots, leaves, fruit, birds, birds' eggs and insects.
Breeding: Gestation 180-193 days. 1-2 young born at a time.
Status: Insufficiently known. Probably vulnerable or endangered. Hunted for
superstitious reasons and the perceived medicinal value of its anatomy.
Similar species: Slender Loris (with slender body and limbs, found only in S India and
Sri Lanka). Not featured in this book.

2. ASSAM MACAQUE *(Plate 1)*
Macaca assamensis

Identification: Head and body 53-68 cm. Tail 19-38 cm. Chunky
macaque. Brownish grey, without a red patch on rump.
Habitat: Hill forests (600-1,800 metres elevation) and mangrove
swamps.
Range: C and E Himalaya, and the Sunderbans (India and Bangladesh).
Behaviour: Diurnal. Generally shy. Gregarious. Runs and walks on all four feet
(quadrupedal movement). Spends a lot of time in trees. Makes a musical 'pio'. Stores
food in cheek pouches to be eaten later. Raids cultivated areas near villages.
Diet: Shoots, leaves, flowers, fruit and insects. Also agricultural crops.
Breeding: Gestation about 165 days. 1 young born at a time.
Status: Common in many parts of its range. Hunted for food and for the medicinal
properties of its flesh.
Similar species: Rhesus Macaque. Bonnet macaque.

3. RHESUS MACAQUE *(Plate 1)*
Macaca mulatta

Identification: Head and body 45-60 cm. Tail 15-30 cm. Brown or
grey-brown, with distinctive orange-red patch on rump.
Habitat: Forest edges, open areas, in or near villages, towns, temples,
railway stations and ruins. Up to 2,400 metres elevation in the Himalaya.
Range: North India, south to the Godavari and Tapti rivers and beyond, Nepal, Bhutan,
Assam, Bangladesh and N Pakistan.

10

Behaviour: Diurnal. Generally shy in forested areas, but often bold in urban areas. Walks and runs on all four feet. Feeds in trees and on the ground. Gregarious. Good swimmer. Troops of up to 50 or more animals. Stores food in cheek pouches to be eaten later. Barks, screeches and grunts.
Diet: Insects, shoots, fruit and seeds. Also cultivated crops and small animals.
Breeding: Gestation about 165 days. 1 young born at a time.
Status: Abundant. Relatively large populations still occur. Rural entertainers train them for village shows.
Similar species: Assam Macaque. Bonnet macaque.

---

4. BONNET MACAQUE *(Plate 1)*
Macaca radiata

Identification: Head and body 35-60 cm. Tail longer than head and body, 48-69 cm. Brown grey to olive brown. Less stocky than the Rhesus Macaque. Distinctive bonnet of long hair on its head, with a centre parting over the forehead.
Habitat: Forests, open areas, in or near villages and towns.
Range: S India, south of a rough line from Bombay to the Godavari river.
Behaviour: Diurnal. Walks and runs on all four feet. More arboreal than the Rhesus Macaque. Good swimmer. Gregarious, lives in troops of up to 40 or more animals. Shy in forested areas, bold in human habitation. Stores food in cheek pouches to be eaten later. Soft grunts, throaty 'krrr' and bird-like 'pio', similar to Liontail Macaque.
Diet: Insects, grubs, spiders, birds' eggs, leaves, shoots and fruit. Also cultivated crops.
Breeding: Gestation presumed 165 days (similar to Rhesus Macaque). 1 young born at a time.
Status: Abundant.
Similar species: Assam Macaque. Rhesus Macaque.

---

5. LIONTAIL MACAQUE *(Plate 1)*
Macaca silenus

Identification: Head and body 40-60 cm. Tail 25-39 cm. Chunky macaque. Black coat contrasts with its distinctive greyish mane of long hair. The tail tuft is similar to that of Lion.
Habitat: Evergreen tropical hill forests from 300 to 1,300 metres elevation; also near cardamom and tea plantations.
Range: Western Ghats of SW India (parts of Kerala, Tamilnadu and Karnataka).
Behaviour: Diurnal. Extremely shy of man. Largely arboreal. Gregarious, in troops of up to 20 or more animals. Walks and runs on all four feet. Feeds in trees and on the ground. Stores food in cheek pouches to be eaten later. Calls - 'coo', 'coyeh' and 'pio'.
Diet: Leaves, shoots, flowers, fruit, seeds, insects and grubs.
Breeding: Gestation 6 months. 1-2 young born at a time.
Status: Endangered. Threatened by the loss of habitat and hunting for its fur and medicinal properties of its anatomy. Population a few thousand.
Similar species: None.

6. HOOLOCK GIBBON (WHITE-BROWED GIBBON)
(Plate 1)
Hylobates hoolock

Identification: Head and body 45-63 cm. Height 90 cm when upright. No tail. Arms are twice the length of the legs and touch the ground when standing upright. Adult males and young of both sexes black, adult females yellow-grey. Distinctive white brows. The only ape found in the subcontinent.
Habitat: Evergreen to moist deciduous hill forests.
Range: NE India and Bangladesh.
Behaviour: Largely arboreal. Diurnal. Feeds mainly during the mornings and late afternoons. Found in small family groups of up to 6 or more animals. Communicates with other groups by making loud howling noises ('whoopoo') in the early mornings and the late afternoons. Territorial. Moves by arm-swinging or brachiation (unique to gibbons and siamangs), often leaping in this manner from branch to branch. Walks or runs on hind feet on larger branches.
Diet: Leaves, shoots, fruit, birds' eggs, insects, grubs and spiders.
Breeding: Gestation 7 months. 1 young born at a time.
Status: Endangered/vulnerable. Main threats from habitat loss and hunting for food.
Similar species: None.

7. HANUMAN LANGUR (BLACK-FACED, GREY OR COMMON LANGUR)
(Plate 1)
Presbytis entellus

RANTH

Identification: Head and body 41-78 cm. Tail 69-108 cm. Grey coat and black face. Slender body, long limbs.
Habitat: Forests, from plains up to 3,600 metres elevation in the Himalaya, open areas, villages and towns.
Range: India, Nepal, Bhutan, Bangladesh, Sri Lanka and N Pakistan.
Behaviour: More arboreal than the Rhesus Macaque. Spends considerable time on the ground foraging and visiting salt licks. Diurnal. Walks and runs on all four feet. Leaps with the hind limbs and lands on fore and hind limbs. Active mainly in the early mornings and late afternoons. Gregarious. Found in one-male and multi-male troops of up to 15 or more (even 100 plus) animals. Sex ratio of 2-6 females for every male. Generally shy, bold in towns and villages. Calls 'whoops', 'kha-ko-kha' and bird-like chirrups. Frequently associates with herds of Chital deer who feed on twigs and leaves dropped from the trees. Also mingles with Rhesus Macaque and Bonnet Macaque.
Diet: Shoots, leaves, flowers, buds and fruit. Occasionally raids cultivation.
Breeding: Gestation about 196-210 days. 1 young born at a time.
Status: Abundant. Protected in the Hindu regions as it is regarded as the Monkey-God, Hanuman, from the Hindu epic, Ramayana, hence the name.
Similar species: Capped Langur. Golden Leaf Monkey.

12

8. GOLDEN LEAF MONKEY (GOLDEN LANGUR)
(Plate 1)
Presbytis geei

Identification: Head and body 50-75 cm. Tail 70-100 cm. Coat
light to dark golden, face black. Slim, long-limbed monkey with tassellated tail, especially
in males.
Habitat: Forests, from plains to 2,400 metres elevation in the Himalaya.
Range: S Bhutan and NE India (in Assam, between the Sankosh river in the west and
the Manas river in the east).
Behaviour: Diurnal. Mainly active in the early mornings and evenings. Walks and runs
on all four feet. Leaps with the hind limbs and lands on fore and hind limbs. Troop sizes
of 4-40 animals. Shy.
Diet: Shoots, leaves, flowers and fruit.
Breeding: Presumed similar to Hanuman Langur.
Status: Vulnerable/endangered. Approximate population of 1,200 in Bhutan and 200 in
India. Mainly threatened by its low numbers and restricted range.
Similar species: Hanuman Langur. Capped Langur.

---

9. NILGIRI LANGUR *(Plate 1)*
Presbytis johnii

Identification: Head and body 60-70 cm. Tail 75-96 cm. Slim monkey
with long limbs. Coat black, with yellow-brown on back of head.
Habitat: Moist deciduous and evergreen forests or 'sholas' between 900
and 2,100 metres elevation. Also near cultivation.
Range: SW India (Nilgiri, Annaimalai and Palni hills).
Behaviour: Diurnal. Walks and runs on all four feet. Leaps with the hind limbs and
lands on fore and hind limbs. Shy of man. Largely arboreal. Found in troops of 3-25
animals. Calls "hoo, hoo, hoo".
Diet: Shoots, leaves, flowers, fruit and seeds. Raids agricultural crops, including
cardamom fields and orchards.
Breeding: Presumed similar to Hanuman Langur.
Status: Endangered. Population of a few hundred. Threatened by deforestation and
hunting for fur, skins (for drums) and flesh (believed to have medicinal and aphrodisiac
properties).
Similar species: Purple-faced Leaf Monkey (Presbytis vetulus), found in Sri Lanka. Not
featured in this book.

---

10. CAPPED LEAF MONKEY *(Plate 1)*
Presbytis pileatus

Identification: Head and body 50-70 cm. Tail 75-105 cm. Slender,
long-limbed monkey. Dark grey upperparts, paler underparts. Long
backward-facing hair on crown gives it a "capped" appearance. Blackish terminal half of tail.
Habitat: Deciduous and evergreen hill forests up to 1,500 metres elevation.
Range: NE India and Bangladesh.

Behaviour: Diurnal. Shy. Predominantly arboreal. Hides behind foliage when disturbed. Walks and runs on all four feet. Leaps with the hind limbs and lands on fore and hind limbs. Found in troops of 8-10 or more animals. Guttural barks and squeals.
Diet: Shoots, leaves, flowers and fruit.
Breeding: Presumed similar to Hanuman Langur.
Status: Vulnerable. Reasonable populations exist in some areas. Main danger from loss of habitat.
Similar species: Hanuman Langur. Golden Leaf Monkey.

---

11. GOLDEN JACKAL *(Plate 2)*
Canis aureus

Identification: Head and body 60-75 cm. Tail 20-25 cm. Shoulder height 38-43 cm. Golden, tan or buff, with a mixture of black; pale underparts. Black-tipped bushy tail.
Habitat: Forests, scrub, deserts, near villages and towns, from plains up to 3,600 metres elevation.
Range: India, Nepal, Bhutan, Bangladesh, Sri Lanka and Pakistan.
Behaviour: Mainly nocturnal and crepuscular. Found singly, in pairs or small family packs. Howls, often taken up in chorus, and yelps. Lives in a hole in the ground or man-made drains and canals. Said to pair for life. Male helps in the upbringing of the young.
Diet: Fruit, birds, reptiles, grubs, small mammals, carrion, plantations (sugar cane, coffee, etc) and poultry.
Breeding: Gestation 60-63 days. 1 litter a year. 3-9 young born at a time. Longevity 8-12 years.
Status: Common. Threatened by hunting for its skin.
Similar species: Wolf.

---

12. WOLF *(Plate 2)*
Canis lupus

Identification: Head and body 90-105 cm. Tail 35-40 cm. Shoulder height 65-75 cm. Sandy, yellow, grey or black (in Himalaya); paler underparts. Tail with black tip.
Habitat: Scrub, open terrain, semi-deserts and high mountains.
Range: Parts of India (N, W and S to Karnataka), Nepal, Bhutan, Bangladesh and Pakistan.
Behaviour: Mainly nocturnal. Generally shy, but may prowl in villages and towns at night, especially if natural food is scarce. Found singly, in pairs, or small family groups. Howls and yaps. Efficient pack hunter.
Diet: Small to medium-sized mammals, birds, carrion and fruit. Also, poultry and livestock (mainly sheep and goat).
Breeding: Gestation 60-63 days. 1 litter a year. 3-10 young born at a time. Longevity 10-16 years.
Status: Vulnerable. Persecuted throughout its range for its fur and as vermin. Easily seen in certain areas in W Rajasthan and Rann of Kutch.
Similar species: Golden Jackal.

13. BENGAL FOX *(Plate 2)*
Vulpes bengalensis

Identification: Head and body 45-60 cm. Tail 25-35 cm. Slender.
Grey, rufous limbs, black-tipped tail.
Habitat: Open lowland terrain, scrub and near human habitation, up to 1,350 metres
elevation. Dislikes dense forests.
Range: Most parts of India, Nepal, Bhutan, Bangladesh and Pakistan.
Behaviour: Nocturnal and diurnal. Shy of man. Found singly, in **pairs**, or small family
groups. Yelps. Den a hole in the ground. Communal dens found.
Diet: Small mammals, reptiles, insects (partial to termites in flight), grubs and fruit.
Occasionally poultry.
Breeding: Gestation 50-53 days. 1 litter a year. 3-4 young born at a time. Longevity
not known.
Status: Common (but seldom seen). Hunted for its fur and for the perceived medicinal
and superstitious properties of its flesh and bones.
Similar species: Red Fox.

---

14. RED FOX *(Plate 2)*
Vulpes vulpes

Identification: Head and body 49-65 cm. Tail 45-50 cm. Handsome
fox, especially in its luxuriant winter coat. Reddish above, with white
underparts and tip of tail.
Habitat: Open mountainous terrain, between 1,000 and 3,000 metres elevation, lowland
stony deserts and in highland cultivation.
Range: Karakoram and Himalaya (Kashmir to Sikkim), NW India and Pakistan.
Behaviour: Nocturnal, occasionally diurnal. Shy of man. Found singly, in pairs or
family groups. Yips, screams, barks, chatters and whines. Den a burrow in the ground.
Males help in the upbringing of the young. Territorial. Communal dens found.
Diet: Small mammals, especially rodents, insects, larvae, worms, carrion, fruit and poultry.
Breeding: Gestation 60-63 days. 1 litter a year. 4-7 young born at a time. Longevity
6-13 years.
Status: Uncommon. Persecuted for its rich fur. Dwindling numbers.
Similar species: Bengal Fox.

---

15. DHOLE (RED OR INDIAN WILD DOG)
(Plate 2)
Cuon alpinus

Identification: Head and body 90 cm. Tail 40-43 cm. Shoulder
height 40-55 cm. Red to tawny; black-tipped bushy tail.
Habitat: Forests in the plains (partial to dense cover, like the Tiger) and in relatively open
terrain in the high Himalaya, up to 3,000 metres elevation or more.
Range: India, Nepal, Bhutan, Bangladesh and Pakistan.
Behaviour: Mainly diurnal. Shy of man. Found in packs of up to 20 or more animals.
Whistles, whimpers, barks and yaps. Formidable pack hunter and will even enter water
(rivers, streams and lakes) in pursuit of cornered quarry. Den a hole in the ground or

among rocks. Communal latrine sites communicate presence of a resident pack.
Diet: Small and medium-sized mammals, like deer; occasionally larger mammals like Gaur and Water Buffalo.
Breeding: Gestation 60-70 days. 1 litter a year. 4-8 young born at a time.
Status: Vulnerable. Reasonable populations are restricted to protected areas.
Similar species: None.

---

16. ASIATIC BLACK BEAR (HIMALAYAN BLACK BEAR) *(Plate 2)*
Selenarctos thibetanus

Identification: Head and body 140-165 cm. Tail vestigial. Chunky, powerfully built bear. Glossy black coat contrasts with white to buff "V" or "U"-shaped mark on breast. Large paws. Claws black.
Habitat: Forests, from the plains to 3,600 metres elevation; also open rocky areas.
Range: Himalaya, N and NE India, Nepal, Bhutan and Pakistan.
Behaviour: Mainly nocturnal, occasionally diurnal. Shy of man. Found singly, in pairs, or small family groups. Agile tree-climber. Den in burrows and tree hollows. Seasonal altitudinal migration in search of food.
Diet: Fruit, honey, carrion and agricultural crops. Also domestic sheep and cattle.
Breeding: Gestation 7-8 months. 1 litter a year. 2-4 young born at a time. Longevity up to 24 years.
Status: Vulnerable/endangered.
Similar species: Sloth bear. Brown Bear.

---

17. BROWN BEAR *(Plate 2)*
Ursus arctos

Identification: Head and body 140-200 cm. Tail 6-8 cm (vestigial). Dark to light brown, powerfully built carnivore.
Habitat: Alpine meadows in the Himalaya, usually between the tree line and the snow line.
Range: NW Pakistan (Karakoram), W and C Himalaya, and Bhutan.
Behaviour: Diurnal and nocturnal. Shy. Found singly, in pairs, or small family groups. Den in caves or tree hollows. Does not normally climb trees. Hibernates during the winter. Seasonal altitudinal migration in search of food.
Diet: Small mammals, fruit, cultivated crops, carrion, livestock, insects, roots and tubers.
Breeding: Gestation 7-8 months. 1-3 young born at a time. Longevity 20-25 years.
Status: Vulnerable. Hunted for fur, flesh, fat and the gall bladder for its perceived medicinal properties.
Similar species: Asiatic Black Bear. Sloth Bear.

---

18. SLOTH BEAR *(Plate 2)*
Melursus ursinus

Identification: Head and body 140-170 cm. Shoulder height 60-90 cm. Tail vestigial. Black, very occasionally brown, shaggy coat (not shiny and smooth like the Asiatic Black Bear). White to yellowish "V" or "U" mark on breast. White to yellowish muzzle and claws.

Habitat: Forests and rocky terrain, from the Himalayan foothills to the plains.

Range: India, Nepal, Bhutan, Bangladesh and Sri Lanka.

Behaviour: Nocturnal and diurnal. Shy. Agile tree climber in search of food. Found singly, in pairs, or mother and 1-2 cubs. Barks and wails. Den in hollows in the ground, rocks or trees. Excellent sense of smell, but poor sight and hearing. Dangerous (especially a mother with young). Mother carries young cubs on back. Known to feed on the sweet juice of Toddy palm and the alcohol-rich flowers of Mahuwa.

Diet: Termites, insects, grubs, honey, carrion, fruit, flowers, roots, grass shoots and cultivated crops (eg sugar cane).

Breeding: Gestation 7 months. 1-3 young born at a time. Longevity up to 30 years.

Status: Vulnerable. Occasionally village entertainers train it for "bear shows". Also hunted for the perceived medicinal properties of its bile.

Similar species: Black bear. Brown Bear.

19. RED PANDA (LESSER PANDA) *(Plate 2)*
Ailurus fulgens

Identification: Head and body 50- 65 cm. Tail 28-48 cm. Chestnut upperparts and tail with darkish rings. Underparts and limbs dark to black. Feet with hairy soles. Short white muzzle and rounded head. Handsome creature, with a masked, raccoon-like face.

Habitat: Temperate forests (partial to bamboo) from 1,500 to 3,500 metres elevation in the Himalaya.

Range: Nepal, Bhutan and E Himalaya.

Behaviour: Nocturnal and crepuscular. Shy. Found singly, in pairs or small family groups. Spends the day in trees. Whistles, squeaks and chirps. Den in tree hollows or rock crevices.

Diet: Shoots, including bamboo, leaves, grasses, fruit, roots, insects, grubs and birds' eggs.

Breeding: Gestation 112-158 days (delayed implantation occurs). 1-4 young born at a time. Longevity 10-14 years.

Status: Insufficiently known. Possibly endangered or vulnerable. Hunted for its attractive fur. Occasionally tamed as pets.

Similar species: None.

20. YELLOW-BELLIED WEASEL *(Plate 3)*
Mustela kathiah

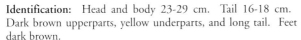

Identification: Head and body 23-29 cm. Tail 16-18 cm. Dark brown upperparts, yellow underparts, and long tail. Feet dark brown.

Habitat: Mountains.

Range: W, C and E Himalaya, between 1,000 and 2,000 metres elevation.

Behaviour: Presumed similar to the Himalayan Weasel.

Diet: Small mammals, especially rodents, birds, birds' eggs and reptiles.

Breeding: Not much is known about its breeding habits.

Status: Insufficiently known.

Similar species: Pale Weasel (Mountain Weasel). Ermine (brown upperparts, white underparts, black tip of tail; all white in the winter, with black tip of tail). Not featured in this book.

---

21. HIMALAYAN WEASEL *(Plate 3)*
Mustela sibirica

Identification: Head and body 30 cm. Tail 15 cm. Reddish or brown, including
bushy tail. Muzzle white or black. Some white on chin and throat.
Habitat: Forests, meadows and open areas in the mountains, between 1,500 and 4,800 metres elevation.
Range: W, C and E Himalaya.
Behaviour: Nocturnal and diurnal. Shy. Found singly, in pairs or in small family groups. Den in hollows in the ground or trees. In villages some inhabit human houses and shelter in the roofs, holes and under the floor boards.
Diet: Small mammals, rodents, birds, birdsí eggs, reptiles, insects and poultry.
Breeding: Gestation 35-42 days. 4 or more litters a year.
Status: Insufficiently known. Hunted for its fur.
Similar species: Beech Marten.

---

22. MOUNTAIN WEASEL (PALE WEASEL) *(Plate 3)*
Mustela altaica

Identification: Head and body 22-29 cm. Tail 11-15 cm. Brown upperparts, yellowish underparts. Feet white, tail without a black tip.
Habitat: Mountains, from 2,100 to 3,900 metres elevation.
Range: Himalaya.
Behaviour: Not much is known of its behaviour.
Diet: Small mammals, birds and reptiles.
Breeding: Gestation 30-49 days. Usually 1-2 or more litters a year.
Status: Insufficiently known.
Similar species: Yellow-bellied Weasel.

---

23. YELLOW-THROATED MARTEN
(Plate 3)
Martes flavigula

Identification: Head and body 45-60 cm. Tail 38-43 cm.
Handsome weasel. Black or dark brown mixed with yellow, with a distinctive yellow throat patch. In the Nilgiris dark brown with reddish forequarters, regarded by some as a separate species, the Nilgiri Marten (Martes gwatkinsi).
Habitat: Forests, from the plains to the treeline at 2,700 metres elevation. In the Nilgiris, above 900 metres elevation.
Range: Himalaya. Also extreme S India, in and around the Nilgiris.
Behaviour: Diurnal and nocturnal. Shy of man. Solitary, but occasionally seen in pairs or small family groups. Excellent tree climber. Den a hole in tree or ground.
Diet: Small mammals, birds, eggs, reptiles, carrion, flowers, fruit and honey.

Breeding: Gestation 5-6 months (including delayed implantation).
Status: Insufficiently known. Probably vulnerable or endangered.
Similar species: None.

24. BEECH MARTEN (STONE MARTEN)

(Plate 3)
Martes foina

Identification: Head and body 25-45 cm. Tail 12-20 cm. Dark or brown upperparts. White throat patch (absent in some).
Habitat: Temperate forests above 1,500 metres elevation, alpine meadows and above the tree line, in or near villages.
Range: Himalaya.
Behaviour: Nocturnal and diurnal. Agile tree climbers. Shy. Normally solitary, occasionally seen in pairs and small family groups. Den a hole in the ground, among rocks or in trees. Growls, squeaks, chatters and screams.
Diet: Small mammals, birds, reptiles, fruit, honey, poultry and insects.
Breeding: Gestation 9 weeks. Extended through delayed implantation to 8-9 months. 1 litter a year. 4-5 young born at a time.
Status: Insufficiently known. Occasionally kept as pets. Hunted for fur.
Similar species: Himalayan Weasel.

25. RATEL (HONEY BADGER) *(Plate 3)*

Mellivora capensis

Identification: Head and body 60-77 cm. Tail 15-20 cm. Shoulder
height 25-30 cm. Muscular bear-like creature with a compact body and powerful limbs. Dark brown or black, with contrasting silvery grey or whitish upperparts from the forehead to beyond the base of tail.
Habitat: Forests, scrubs and stony deserts.
Range: From the Himalayan foothills south in most parts of India, Nepal and Pakistan.
Behaviour: Largely nocturnal, occasionally diurnal. Shy and rarely seen. Aggressive when threatened and fearless against bigger adversaries, being armed with sharp teeth, tough, loose hide, and large stink glands. Mother carries young on back. Den a burrow; in dry areas near stream beds. Prodigious digger. Can climb trees.
Diet: Small mammals, birds, reptiles, carrion, fruit, honey and poultry.
Breeding: Gestation 6 months. 1 litter a year. 2 young born at a time. Longevity 24 years.
Status: Insufficiently known.
Similar species: None.

26. EURASIAN OTTER (COMMON OTTER)

(Plate 3)
Lutra lutra

Identification: Head and body 60-70 cm. Tail 35-40 cm. Robust muscular body, thick tail. Dark or light brown, grizzled upperparts,

whitish on lower muzzle and throat.
Habitat: Rivers, ponds and lakes in hills and mountains up to 3,600 metres elevation.
Range: Himalaya and adjoining areas, S India and Sri Lanka.
Behaviour: Mainly nocturnal, also diurnal. Shy. Territorial. Group size 1-6. Hunts mainly in the water. Seasonal altitudinal migration in search of food. Can travel long distances overland. Den in the ground near water's edge, usually among roots of trees, with at least one opening under water. Whistles, chirps and squeaks.
Diet: Mainly fish, also frogs, crustaceans and water birds.
Breeding: Gestation 61-65 days. 1 litter a year. 1-5 young born at a time. Longevity up to 20 years.
Status: Uncommon.
Similar species: Smooth-coated Otter. Oriental Small-clawed Otter.

27. SMOOTH-COATED OTTER (SMOOTH INDIAN OTTER) *(Plate 3)*
Lutra perspicillata

Identification: Head and body 65-75 cm. Tail 40-45 cm. Chunky, with muscular tail. Light or dark brown, paler underparts, upperparts not grizzled as in the Eurasian Otter. Lower muzzle and throat whitish.
Habitat: Rivers, lakes, canals, including arid areas and low hills; also coastal waters and thick forests.
Range: Much of India, Nepal, Bhutan, Bangladesh and Pakistan.
Behaviour: Diurnal and nocturnal. Shy. Group size 2-10. Excellent swimmers and strong walkers covering considerable distances over land. Often hunts in groups. Den in a burrow, near water. Barks and whistles.
Diet: Mainly fish, but also frogs and birds.
Breeding: Gestation 63-65 days. 1-4 young born at a time.
Status: Insufficiently known. Probably vulnerable or endangered. In Orissa (India), trained otters are used by fishermen to drive fish into nets and in Sind (Pakistan) to attract dolphins.
Similar species: Eurasian Otter. Oriental Small-clawed Otter.

28. ORIENTAL SMALL-CLAWED OTTER *(Plate 3)*
Aonyx cinerea

Identification: Head and body 45-64 cm. Tail 25-35 cm. Brown upperparts, paler underparts. Whitish lower muzzle and throat. Feet webbed to about the last joint of toes and with rudimentary claws.
Habitat: Rivers, lakes, estuaries and flooded rice fields.
Range: Foothills of the W, C and E Himalaya, NE India and Bangladesh. Also in the higher hills of S India (Coorg, Nilgiri and Palni).
Behaviour: Presumed similar to the other otters of the subcontinent. Groups size of up to 18 animals.
Diet: Crabs, molluscs, other aquatic creatures and fish.
Breeding: Gestation 60-64 days. 1-6 young born at a time.
Status: Insufficiently known. Probably vulnerable or endangered.
Similar species: Eurasian Otter. Smooth-coated Otter.

29. SMALL INDIAN CIVET *(Plate 3)*
Viverricula indica

Identification: Head and body 60 cm. Tail 30 cm. Grey, with dark spots in rows on the flanks and dark rings on the tail. No dorsal crest.
Habitat: Near villages and towns, scrub, grasslands and forests. Avoids dense vegetation.
Range: India, Nepal, Bhutan, Bangladesh, Sri Lanka and Pakistan. Also in the foothills of the Himalaya.
Behaviour: Mainly nocturnal. Shy. Den in tree holes or burrows or in urban drains. Seen singly, in pairs or small family groups. Clicks and meows.
Diet: Small mammals, birds, reptiles, insects and fruit; occasionally poultry.
Breeding: 4-5 young born at a time.
Status: Insufficiently known. Occasionally kept as pets to get rid of vermin.
Similar species: Large Indian Civet.

30. LARGE INDIAN CIVET *(Plate 3)*
Viverra zibetha

Identification: Head and body 80 cm. Tail 45 cm. Grey, with small dark spots on the body. Bold dark bands on tail and on neck and shoulders. Dorsal crest of erectile dark hair (lacking in the Small Indian Civet).
Habitat: Forest and scrub.
Range: Nepal, Bhutan, NE India and Bangladesh.
Behaviour: Nocturnal. Normally solitary. Shy. Den in a burrow.
Diet: Small mammals, reptiles, birds, insects, poultry, fruit and vegetables.
Breeding: 3-4 young born at a time. Longevity 12-15 years.
Status: Insufficiently known.
Similar species: Small Indian Civet.

31. SPOTTED LINSANG
(TIGER CIVET) *(Plate 4)*
Prionodon pardicolor

Identification: Head and body 35-37 cm. Tail 28-34 cm. Elongated body, short limbs and a pointed muzzle. Golden brown with large black spots and black ringed tail. Unmistakable.
Habitat: Hill forests up to 1,800 metres elevation.
Range: E Nepal, Bhutan and NE India. Recent records from N India (Corbett National Park).
Behaviour: Nocturnal. Shy. Mainly solitary. Active tree climber. Den a hollow in trees.
Diet: Small mammals, birds, fruit and insects.
Breeding: 2 litters a year. 2 young born at a time.
Status: Endangered.
Similar species: None.

32. THREE-STRIPED PALM CIVET *(Plate 4)*
Arctogalidea trivirgata

Identification: Head and body 43-53 cm. Tail 51-66 cm. Dark grey to grey-brown upperparts, yellowish belly, 3 dark dorsal stripes. Long, partly prehensile tail.
Habitat: Forests.
Range: NE India.
Behaviour: Nocturnal. Arboreal. Shy.
Diet: Small mammals, birds, reptiles, insects and fruit.
Breeding: Gestation 45 days. 1-2 litters a year. 2-3 young born at a time. Longevity 10-12 years.
Status: Uncommon.
Similar species: Common Palm Civet. Masked Palm Civet.

33. COMMON PALM CIVET (TODDY CAT) *(Plate 4)*
Paradoxurus hermaphroditus

Identification: Head and body 42-69 cm. Tail 46 cm. Blackish, including limbs. Black head with white markings. Occasionally dorsal stripes or spots.
Habitat: Forests, scrub, plantations, villages and cities.
Range: India, Nepal, Bhutan, Bangladesh, Sri Lanka and Pakistan. Not in desert areas.
Behaviour: Mainly nocturnal. Arboreal, increasingly terrestrial. Den either a hole in tree or the ground, or in human dwellings in roofs, under floor boards and drains.
Diet: Small mammals, birds, reptiles, insects, poultry, fruit & plantations. Fond of Toddy juice, hence also referred to as the Toddy Cat.
Breeding: 3-4 young born at a time.
Status: Common. Occasionally kept as pets.
Similar species: Three-striped Palm Civet. Masked Palm Civet.

34. MASKED PALM CIVET (HIMALAYAN PALM CIVET) *(Plate 4)*
Paguma larvata

Identification: Head and body 60 cm. Tail 60 cm. Dark grey upperparts, whitish underparts.
Habitat: Hill and mountain forests.
Range: Himalaya, NE India and the Andaman Islands.
Behaviour: Nocturnal. Arboreal, but also hunts on the ground. Den a hole in trees.
Diet: Mainly fruit; also, small mammals and birds.
Breeding: 3-4 young born at a time.
Status: Uncommon.
Similar species: Three-striped Palm Civet. Common Palm Civet.

35. BINTURONG (BEAR CAT) *(Plate 4)*
Arctictis binturong

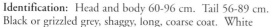

Identification: Head and body 60-96 cm. Tail 56-89 cm.
Black or grizzled grey, shaggy, long, coarse coat. White
tufted edges to the ears and whiskers. Prehensile tail with a thick base.
Habitat: Tropical foothill forests up to 2,000 metres elevation.
Range: C and E Himalaya (Nepal, Bhutan and NE India).
Behaviour: Nocturnal. Secretive. Arboreal, with slow movements, the prehensile tail
aiding its balance. Found singly or in pairs. Den a hole in trees. Grunts and hisses.
Diet: Small mammals, reptiles, birds, carrion, insects and fruit.
Breeding: Gestation 92 days. 1-3 young born at a time.
Status: Endangered. Danger from habitat loss.
Similar species: None.

36. SMALL INDIAN MONGOOSE *(Plate 4)*
Herpestes auropunctatus

Identification: Head and body 25-30 cm. Tail 20-25 cm. Dark
or pale golden brown. Elongate, low-slung body, with short limbs.
Habitat: Woodlands, cultivation and near villages.
Range: N and E India, Nepal, Bhutan and Pakistan.
Behaviour: Diurnal. Shy. Group size of 1-4 animals. Den in a burrow. Purrs.
Diet: Small mammals, reptiles, birds and insects.
Breeding: Gestation 7 weeks. 1-3 or more litters a year. 2-3 young born at a time.
Longevity 7-8 years.
Status: Common. Often kept as pets to get rid of vermin in homes. Snake charmers keep
them to entertain villagers with mongoose-cobra shows. The excited cobra spreads its
hood and strikes at the mongoose who is too agile for the snake.
Similar species: Indian Grey Mongoose. Ruddy Mongoose.

37. INDIAN GREY MONGOOSE *(Plate 4)*
Herpestes edwardsii

Identification: Head and body 40-45 cm. Tail 40-45 cm. Yellow
grey, grizzled. Tail tipped white or yellowish.
Habitat: Scrub forest, desert, cultivation, open terrain, villages and cities.
Range: India, Nepal, Bhutan, Bangladesh, Sri Lanka and Pakistan.
Behaviour: Diurnal and nocturnal. Group size 1-4. Den a hole in the base of trees
or in the ground, drains, or roofs of houses. Usually comes off best in fights with cobras
due to its agility and its erectile fur which makes the snake miss the flesh.
Diet: Small mammals, reptiles, birds, birds' eggs, insects, poultry, carrion, fruit and roots.
Breeding: Gestation 60 days. Up to 5 litters a year. 2-4 young born at a time. Longevity
7-8 years.
Status: Common.
Similar species: Small Indian Mongoose. Ruddy Mongoose.

38. RUDDY MONGOOSE *(Plate 4)*
Herpestes smithii

Identification: Head and body 40-45 cm. Tail 40-45 cm. Generally ruddy. Black tip to tail.
Habitat: Forests and scrub.
Range: C and S India, and Sri Lanka.
Behaviour: Presumed similar to the Indian Grey Mongoose.
Diet: Small mammals, birds and reptiles.
Breeding: Longevity up to 17 years.
Status: Insufficiently known.
Similar species: Small Indian Mongoose. Indian Grey Mongoose.

---

39. CRAB-EATING MONGOOSE *(Plate 4)*
Herpestes urva

Identification: Head and body 45-50 cm. Tail 25-30 cm. Metallic grey, coarse fur, tip of tail hairless. Distinctive white stripe on either side of neck.
Habitat: Hill forests near water.
Range: Nepal, NE India and Bangladesh.
Behaviour: Diurnal and nocturnal. Shy. Hunts in water and on land. Group size 1-4. Den in a burrow. Squirts a fluid from the anal glands in defense.
Diet: Fish, frogs, crabs and other small creatures.
Breeding: Longevity 10 years.
Status: Insufficiently known.
Similar species: Stripe-necked Mongoose.

---

40. STRIPE-NECKED MONGOOSE *(Plate 4)*
Herpestes vitticollis

Identification: Head and body 40-45 cm. Tail 40-45 cm. Chunky. Reddish grey with black tip to tail. Distinctive black neck stripe.
Habitat: Forests, open scrub, cultivation and near villages. Along water courses and swamps.
Range: SW India and Sri Lanka.
Behaviour: Diurnal and crepuscular.
Diet: Small mammals, including Mouse-deer, birds, reptiles and other small creatures.
Breeding: 3 young born at a time. Longevity 13 years.
Status: Insufficiently known.
Similar species: Crab-eating Mongoose.

---

41. STRIPED HYAENA *(Plate 5)*
Hyaena hyaena

Identification: Head and body 100-120 cm. Tail 25-35 cm. Shoulder height 65-80 cm. Large head and shoulders. Erectile dorsal crest. Weak rump. Grey, buff, or yellowish grey coat, with

24

well- defined dark or black stripes on the body and limbs. Tip of tail and much of dorsal crest black. Thin limbs. Forefeet much larger than hindfeet.

Habitat: Broken terrain, scrub, forests (avoids moist dense forests), sugar cane fields and semi-deserts.

Range: Most suitable parts of lowland India, south to the Nilgiri Hills, Nepal, Bangladesh and Pakistan.

Behaviour: Mainly nocturnal. Generally shy. Seen singly, in pairs, or small groups of up to 6 animals. Howls, whines, growls and "cackling laughter". Marks territory with secretions from anal glands. Den a hole or cavity in rocks, ground or under trees. Can crush and digest large bones, its droppings usually turning white (calcium) with age.

Diet: Small and medium sized mammals, birds, reptiles, carrion and small livestock. Both scavenger and hunter.

Breeding: Gestation 3 months. 2-4 young born at a time. Longevity up to 24 years.

Status: Uncommon. Widely hunted as a pest.

Similar species: None.

42. LEOPARD CAT *(Plate 5)*
Felis bengalensis

Identification: Head and body 60-66 cm. Tail 28-30 cm. Domestic Cat size, with relatively small head and long limbs. Yellow, grey or golden upperparts, white underparts. Large black or brown spots, including on tail.

Habitat: Forests, near villages. From the plains to the Himalayan foothills.

Range: India, Nepal, Bhutan, Bangladesh and N Pakistan.

Behaviour: Nocturnal. Hunts in trees and on the ground. Good swimmer. Solitary or in pairs. Den a hole in tree or small caves.

Diet: Small mammals, birds and poultry.

Breeding: Gestation 56-70 days. 1-4 young born at a time. Longevity 8-15 years. Said to interbreed with domestic cats.

Status: Vulnerable. Hunted for its pelt. Often kept as pets.

Similar species: Fishing Cat. Marbled Cat.

43. CARACAL *(Plate 5)*
Felis caracal

Identification: Head and body 60-82 cm. Tail 20-32 cm. Reddish grey upperparts, buff or white underparts. Lynx-like build, but slighter, with long limbs (hind legs longer than fore). Broad head and distinctive long black tufts on ears. The name Caracal derives from the Turkish "garah gulak" meaning "black ear". No ruff.

Habitat: Open terrain, stony deserts, scrub forests and low hills.

Range: N and C India, and Pakistan.

Behaviour: Nocturnal and crepuscular. Shy. Extremely agile. Good tree climber. Den a hole in tree, rock or ground.

Diet: Small mammals, including young deer and antelope, birds, reptiles and poultry.

Breeding: Gestation 68-78 days. 1-6 young born at a time. Longevity 16-17 years.

Status: Endangered.
Similar species: Eurasian Lynx.

44. JUNGLE CAT *(Plate 5)*
Felis chaus

Identification: Head and body 60 cm. Tail 23-29 cm. Grey upperparts with a touch of yellow or red, light underparts. Short black-ringed tail with a black tip. 2 dark stripes on upper forelimb, 3-4 on the thigh.
Habitat: Forests, scrub, desert, near villages and cultivation. Up to 2,400 metres elevation.
Range: In most parts of India, Nepal, Bhutan, Bangladesh, Sri Lanka and Pakistan.
Behaviour: Diurnal and nocturnal. Shy. Group size 1-4. Den a burrow in the ground. Purrs.
Diet: Small mammals, birds, reptiles and poultry.
Breeding: Gestation 63-68 days. 1-6 young born at a time. Longevity up to 14 years.
Status: Uncommon (although common in some national parks).
Similar species: None.

45. PALLAS'S CAT *(Plate 5)*
Felis manul

Identification: Head and body 50-60 cm. Tail 21-30 cm. Stocky looking. Metallic grey. Occasionally with black cross bands on its distal back. The thick tail has 5-6 black rings and tip. Broad head with ears set wide apart. 2 distinctive black cheek stripes.
Habitat: Transhimalayan deserts, above the tree line, between 3,000 and 4,800 metres elevation.
Range: Ladakh and possibly Himachal Pradesh.
Behaviour: Nocturnal. Secretive. Solitary. Den a hole in the ground or rock. Hisses, snarls and screeches.
Diet: Small mammals like Pikas and birds.
Breeding: Gestation 66-75 days. 1-6 young born at a time. Longevity up to 11 years.
Status: Insufficiently known. Presumed endangered.
Similar species: None.

46. MARBLED CAT *(Plate 5)*
Felis marmorata

Identification: Head and body 45-61 cm. Tail 35-55 cm. Greyish brown, with large "marbled" markings and long tail. Undersides have pale background. Short, spotted limbs with large feet.
Habitat: Forests.
Range: Nepal, Bhutan, NE India and Bangladesh.
Behaviour: Nocturnal. Arboreal. Hunts in trees and on the ground.
Diet: Small mammals and birds.
Breeding: Gestation 77-81 days. 1-4 young born at a time. Longevity up to 12 years.
Status: Endangered. Hunted for its fur.
Similar species: Clouded Leopard.

47. RUSTY-SPOTTED CAT *(Plate 5)*
Felis rubiginosa

Identification: Head and body 35-48 cm. Tail 15-25 cm. Smallest of all cats. Greyish or fawn upperparts, with rusty or brown spots (stripes/bars on the neck and forequarters), whitish underparts with black spots.
Habitat: Forest, scrub, grassland, near villages and ruins.
Range: Isolated pockets in N, C and S India, mainly in the South, and Sri Lanka.
Behaviour: Nocturnal. Arboreal.
Diet: Small mammals, birds, insects and poultry.
Breeding: Gestation 65-69 days. 1-3 young born at a time.
Status: Insufficiently known. Some areas seem to have reasonable numbers.
Similar species: Wild Cat. Fishing Cat.

48. WILD CAT (DESERT CAT) *(Plate 5)*
Felis silvestris/lybica

Identification: Head and body 50-65 cm. Tail 25-30 cm. Yellowish grey upperparts, with sparse dark spots which extend to the tail, the distal half of which is ringed black. White underparts.
Habitat: Desert, scrub forest, savannah and woodland.
Range: W and WC India, and Pakistan.
Behaviour: Nocturnal. Seen singly, in pairs, or small family parties. Meows. Largely hunts on the ground, but a good tree climber. Den a burrow in the ground or cave.
Diet: Small mammals, birds, reptiles, termites, fruit and poultry.
Breeding: Gestation 56-68 days. 2-6 young born at a time.
Status: Endangered. Locally hunted for its fur. Ancestor to and interbreeds with the Domestic Cat.
Similar species: Rusty-spotted Cat. Fishing Cat.

49. ASIATIC GOLDEN CAT *(Plate 5)*
Felis temminckii

Identification: Head and body 73-105 cm. Tail 43-56 cm. Golden brown, grey or red. Handsome, sturdily built cat. Distinctive whitish cheek stripe with dark borders above and below.
Habitat: Hill forests and moist rocky terrain up to 1,500 metres elevation.
Range: Nepal, Bhutan, NE India and Bangladesh.
Behaviour: Good tree climber. Den a hole in trees. Will also shelter in rock crevices.
Diet: Small animals, including small livestock and poultry.
Breeding: Gestation 80 days. 1-3 young born at a time.
Status: Endangered.
Similar species: None.

50. FISHING CAT *(Plate 5)*
Felis viverrina

Identification: Head and body 57-86 cm. Tail 25-32 cm.
Chunky. Brownish grey, with dark spots set roughly in
longitudinal rows. Markings on dorsal part of neck and shoulders are elongated.
Habitat: Dense forest up to 1,500 metres elevation, scrub, grassland, near water, tidal
creeks, mangroves and backwaters.
Range: N and NE India, Nepal, Bhutan, Bangladesh and Sri Lanka; also possibly SW
India and S Pakistan.
Behaviour: Diurnal and nocturnal. Shy. Group size 1-4. Catches fish with its forepaws.
Den a hole in tree or ground.
Diet: Small mammals, birds, fish, molluscs, aquatic creatures, carrion, livestock and insects.
Breeding: Gestation 63-70 days. 1-4 young born at a time. Longevity 12 years.
Status: Vulnerable.
Similar species: Rusty-spotted Cat. Wild Cat.

51. EURASIAN LYNX *(Plate 6)*
Lynx lynx

Identification: Head and body 85-107 cm. Tail 14-23 cm. Chunky,
pale grey, long limbed (hind legs longer than fore), with a short black-
tipped tail, hair tufts on the tips of the ears 4-6 cm long and a conspicuous ruff around
its face.
Habitat: Mountains with cover, between 1,700 and 3,400 metres elevation.
Range: Northern tip of India (Ladakh, Gilgit), N Pakistan and N Nepal.
Behaviour: Nocturnal and diurnal. Numbers usually seen together, 1-3. Largely hunts
on the ground by stalking and ambush. Good tree climber. Purrs. Den a cave or a hole
in rocks.
Diet: Small and medium sized mammals, birds, livestock and carrion.
Breeding: Gestation 60-69 days. 1-4 young born at a time. Longevity up to 24 years.
Status: Endangered.
Similar species: Caracal.

52. LION *(Plate 6)*
Panthera leo

Identification: Head, body and tail 275-290 cm. Shoulder height 80-
110 cm. Yellowish grey upperparts, white or whitish underparts. Tufts
of hair on tail tip, elbow joints and along the belly (fringe). Males have dark manes (less
luxuriant than those of the African Lion). Young are spotted or striped.
Habitat: Dry deciduous forest, scrub and grassland.
Range: Gir in W India.
Behaviour: Nocturnal and diurnal. Social, seen in prides of up to 10 or more animals.
Territorial. Roars and moans. Den in secluded vegetation.
Diet: Mainly large and medium size mammals, including livestock
Breeding: Gestation 105-116 days. 2-5 young born at a time. Longevity 15-30 years.
Status: Endangered. Population approx 300 (refers only to the Asian subspecies,

28

Panthera leo persica).
Similar species: None.

53. LEOPARD *(Plate 6)*
Panthera pardus

Identification: Head, body and tail 215-245 cm. Handsome and lithe. Grey to golden yellow with dark or black rosettes. Small spots on head and lower limbs. Some all-black animals (due to melanism) in S and NE India. The Leopard is also called Panther.
Habitat: Forests, scrub and open terrain, including the Himalaya.
Range: India, Nepal, Bhutan, Bangladesh, Sri Lanka and Pakistan.
Behaviour: Nocturnal and diurnal. Agile tree climber, occasionally carrying its prey to a safe height to protect it from scavengers. Shy. Territorial. Hunts by stalking and pouncing. Found singly, in pairs or small family groups. Den a secluded spot in a thicket. Rasping calls when on heat, grunts and snarls. Monkeys, peafowl, deer and giant and striped squirrels give alarm calls on seeing Leopard.
Diet: Mainly medium-sized mammals like deer and monkey, livestock, carrion, birds and reptiles.
Breeding: Gestation 87-94 days. 2-4 young born at a time. Longevity 15 years.
Status: Uncommon. Possibly vulnerable. Widely persecuted for its fur.
Similar species: Snow Leopard.

54. TIGER *(Plate 6)*
Panthera tigris

Identification: Head, body and tail 260-290 cm. Heavy build. Unmistakable. Yellow, golden or reddish upperparts, white underparts. Distinctive black bold stripes. Unique markings on head and body used for identification of individuals in the wild.
Habitat: Forests and grasslands, up to 3,000 metres elevation, and mangrove swamps.
Range: India, Nepal, Bhutan and Bangladesh.
Behaviour: Mainly nocturnal. Shy and retiring. Usually seen singly, occasionally in pairs or in small family groups of 2-5 animals. Territorial. Communicates through scent marking and vocalisation. Roars, growl, moans and resonant "aonnh". Monkeys, peafowl and deer give alarm call on seeing Tiger. Hunts by stalking and ambush. Den in a thicket.
Diet: Deer, wild boar, monkeys, peafowl and livestock. Animals as large as adult Gaur and Water Buffalo and calves of Indian Rhinoceros. Also smaller mammals, reptiles and amphibians.
Breeding: Gestation 103-112 days. 2-6 young born at a time. Longevity 15-26 years.
Status: Endangered. Estimated population in the subcontinent 3,000-4,000. Hunted for the illegal export of its skins and bones to the Far East for medicinal purposes.
Similar species: None.

55. SNOW LEOPARD *(Plate 6)*
Panthera uncia

Identification: Head and body 100-110 cm. Tail 83-90 cm.
Light grey upperparts, white underparts. Dark spots on head
and lower limbs, rosettes on the body. Short limbs with large feet.
Habitat: Himalayan steppes, scrub, forest and pastures above the tree line. Between 1,800 and 3,600 metres elevation.
Range: W, C and E Himalaya, and Karakoram range in N Pakistan.
Behaviour: Nocturnal and crepuscular. Shy. Den in hollow of rock. Altitudinal migration in search of food.
Diet: Wild goat and sheep, musk deer, small mammals and domestic livestock.
Breeding: Gestation 98-104 days. 1-5 young born at a time. Longevity up to 21 years.
Status: Endangered. Persecuted for its fur. Estimated population 750-1,500.
Similar species: Leopard.

56. CLOUDED LEOPARD *(Plate 6)*
Neofelis nebulosa

Identification: Head and body 75-105 cm. Tail 70-90 cm. Grey
or yellowish brown upperparts, whitish underparts. Distinctive
large dark blotches, often bordered with black, on the body (hence "clouded"). Thick body, large feet, short limbs, long tail.
Habitat: Evergreen forests, occasionally near human settlements.
Range: East Nepal, Bhutan and NE India.
Behaviour: Nocturnal and shy. Hunts in trees and on the ground. Known to pounce upon prey from overhanging branch, hence known as "bandar bagh" (bandar = monkey, bagh = tiger) by some tribal peoples. Den a hollow in a tree.
Diet: Deer and other small to medium sized mammals. Also livestock near villages.
Breeding: Gestation 87-99 days. 1-5 young born at a time. Longevity 11-17 years.
Status: Vulnerable/endangered.
Similar species: Marbled Cat.

57. GANGES DOLPHIN *(Plate 7)*
Platanista gangetica

Identification: Total length 150-245 cm or more. Females larger
than males. Metallic grey, lighter on the underparts. Spindle-
shaped body with a prolonged beak (up to one-fifth of the body
length), rudimentary eyes, hint of a neck, rudimentary dorsal fin, triangular pectoral flippers, and the distinctive dorsally flattened tail flukes of dolphins and whales.
Habitat: Rivers with deep pools.
Range: Ganges, Brahmaputra and Indus river systems, and estuarine waters (but not in the sea).
Behaviour: Surfaces every 30-45 seconds or so to breath with a hiss (which sounds like "sons" or "susu", which give it its local name in many areas). Usually 1-4 seen in a stretch of river. Seasonal migration in some rivers, dictated by the availability of prey. Food is found by echolocation. Best seen near deep undisturbed pools of water. Normally swims

on its side, taking the upright position when surfacing to breathe.
Diet: Catfish, crustaceans and other animals living on the bottom of rivers.
Breeding: Gestation 9-10 months. 1-2 young born at a time. Longevity 28 years.
Status: Vulnerable. Occasionally caught in the nets of local fishermen. Hunted for its flesh and fat. Estimated population 4,000-5,000. Dams across rivers isolate populations.
Similar species: None. Some regard the Indus Dolphin as a separate species (Platanista minor).

58. INDIAN ELEPHANT *(Plate 7)*
Elephas maximus

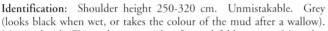

Identification: Shoulder height 250-320 cm. Unmistakable. Grey (looks black when wet, or takes the colour of the mud after a wallow). Massive head. Triangular ears, with a forward fold on top. Muscular, wrinkled, trunk. Thick loose skin. Pillar-like legs. Long tail with tassel of bristles. Males larger, most with tusks (few tuskers in Sri Lanka). No prominent tusks in females, only small tushes.
Habitat: Forests and grasslands, partial to bamboo forests. In hills and mountains up to 3,600 metres elevation.
Range: India, Nepal, Bhutan, Bangladesh and Sri Lanka.
Behaviour: Nocturnal and diurnal. Feeds for up to 16 hours daily, consuming 200+ kg of green fodder. Generally shy. Group sizes of up to 40 or more animals in a family group, led by a matriarch. Young bulls are often found alone, in pairs or all-male herds. Follows regular feeding routes. Squeaks, rumbles, roars and trumpets. Males, and occasionally females, come into "musth" characterised by swollen and leaking temporal glands, unusual aggression, urine dribbling, and heightened sexual activity. Excellent swimmers, known to island-hop in the Andaman Sea. Poor sight, excellent smell and hearing.
Diet: Grasses, bamboo, tree barks, leaves, fruit and flowers. Habitually raids cultivation near villages.
Breeding: Gestation 20-22 months. 1-2 young born at a time. Longevity 60-70 years.
Status: Vulnerable/endangered. Estimated population 17,000-22,000 in India, mainly in the NE, 100 in Nepal and Bhutan, and 300 in Bangladesh. Declining throughout its range from loss of habitat and poaching. Hindus revere the Indian Elephant as an embodiment of Ganesh, the elephant-headed god of good fortune.
Similar species: None.

59. ASIATIC WILD ASS *(Plate 7)*
Equus hemionus

Identification: Shoulder height 110-120 cm. Larger than Domestic Ass (Equus asinus). Reddish grey to pale chestnut upperparts, white underparts. During the summer the red is pronounced against the pale background. Dark mane and dorsal stripe to base of tail. Each limb ends in a single hoof. Ladakh animals, known as Kiang, are bigger, darker and with wider hooves.
Habitat: High ground grassy islands or "bets" in the Rann of Kutch, in the W Indian desert (subject to monsoon flooding), and the dry steppes of the Tibetan Plateau.
Range: Rann of Kutch, Baluchistan, Ladakh and Spiti.
Behaviour: Nocturnal and diurnal. Gregarious, found in groups of up to 60 or more

animals. Avoids man.

Diet: Grasses. Often raids cultivation.

Breeding: Gestation 11 months. 1 young born at a time.

Status: Endangered. Estimated population in W India over 1,500.

Similar species: None. Some regard the Kiang of Ladakh (see above) as a separate species, Equus kiang.

---

60. INDIAN RHINOCEROS *(Plate 7)*
Rhinoceros unicornis

Identification: Shoulder height 155-180 cm. Grey, thick, folded skin, giving it the appearance of being armour-plated. Strong short limbs ending in 3 toes. Single horn (15-30 cm) on top of snout. Prehistoric-looking.

Habitat: Floodplain grasslands and riverine forests.

Range: Foothills of the Himalaya, along the "terai", "dun" valleys and "duars", from Dudhwa, N India, in the west, through Nepal, to Kaziranga in NE India.

Behaviour: Nocturnal and diurnal. Normally solitary, but in open areas 1-10 animals may be seen in loose groups. Whistles, grunts, snorts and rattles. Follows regular paths through thick, almost impassable, tall grass. Habitually defecates at latrine sites which over time become large dung middens.

Diet: Grasses, leaves, shoots and cultivation.

Breeding: Gestation 16 months. 1 young born at a time. Longevity 40 years.

Status: Endangered. Estimated population of 1,700-2,000. Persecuted for its horn (more valuable than its weight in gold), skin and other body parts for medicinal and superstitious reasons.

Similar species: Javan Rhinoceros (smaller, until recently found in Bangladesh and NE India, now extinct in the Indian subcontinent). Not featured in this book.

---

61. PYGMY HOG *(Plate 7)*
Sus salvanius

Identification: Shoulder height 25-30 cm. Very short tail (less than 4 cm). Smaller version of the Wild Boar with a rounded rear. Brown to blackish (young with brownish red stripes) coarse hair, no dorsal crest. 3 pairs of teats (6 pairs in Wild Boar).

Habitat: Grasslands and riverine forests.

Range: "Terai" of India and Nepal and the "duars" of Bhutan and Assam. Possibly N and E Bangladesh also.

Behaviour: Group size 5-20 animals. Shy. Mainly nocturnal. Grunts. Den a nest on the ground amongst thick grasses (a shallow depression covered by foliage).

Diet: Grasses, roots, tubers, insects and birds' eggs.

Breeding: Gestation approx 100-120 days. 2-6 young born at a time. Longevity 10-12 years.

Status: Endangered. Population estimated at several hundred.

Similar species: Wild Boar.

62. WILD BOAR *(Plate 7)*
Sus scrofa

Identification: Shoulder height 60-90 cm. Tail 20-30 cm. Black or dark brown. Large head, long snout, with tushes on upper and lower jaws, being larger in males, the longer lower tushes 10-20 cm long. Heavily built with spindly legs. Dorsal crest from nape to back. Newly born animals are brown with black and light longitudinal stripes.
Habitat: Forests, grasslands, scrubs and near cultivation.
Range: India, Nepal, Bhutan, Bangladesh, Sri Lanka and Pakistan.
Behaviour: Nocturnal and diurnal. Gregarious, in groups of up to 30 or more animals. Adult males generally solitary except during the mating period. Fond of wallowing in the mud. Extremely agile. Feeding groups often accompanied by birds such as egrets and mynahs. Excellent sense of smell. Den a shelter in a thicket or tall grass. Grunts and squeals.
Diet: Omnivorous - grasses, roots, tubers, carrion, snakes, insects and cultivated crops.
Breeding: Gestation 4 months. 4-12 young born at a time. Longevity 15-20 years.
Status: Abundant. Good populations in protected areas. Ancestor of the Domestic Pig (Sus domesticus).
Similar species: Pygmy Hog.

63. INDIAN SPOTTED CHEVROTAIN (MOUSE DEER) *(Plate 7)*
Tragulus meminna

Identification: Shoulder height 25-30 cm. Tiny deer-like. Olive brown upperparts speckled with yellow; white underparts. Longitudinal rows of buff or white spots on the flanks merge to form stripes. Limbs end in 4 well-developed toes. No antlers. Tusks in both sexes, larger in males. Rump higher than shoulders.
Habitat: Forests and grasslands in the hills up to 1,850 metres elevation.
Range: India, south of the Himalaya, and Sri Lanka.
Behaviour: Nocturnal and crepuscular. Shy. Solitary or in pairs. Can climb gently-sloping tree trunks. Den in a tree hollow.
Diet: Grasses, leaves and fruit.
Breeding: Gestation 150 days. 1-2 young born at a time.
Status: Insufficiently known. Hunted for food.
Similar species: None.

64. FOREST MUSK DEER *(Plate 8)*
Moschus chrysogaster

Identification: Shoulder height 40-50 cm. Dark brown and grey upperparts, back and flanks, with rows of light spots; paler underparts. Long limbs end in splayed toes and well-developed dew claws. No antlers. Tusks, larger in males. Males with the prized musk glands in front of their genitals. Rump higher than shoulders.
Habitat: Mountain forests between 2,200 and 4,400 metres elevation.
Range: W, C and E Himalaya.
Behaviour: Crepuscular. Shy. Numbers usually seen, 1-3.

Diet: Grass, leaves, lichens, ferns and mosses.
Breeding: Gestation 5-6 months. 1-2 young born at a time. Longevity 13 years.
Status: Vulnerable. Persecuted for its "musk" pods. Musk Deer is also farmed commercially for its "musk".
Similar species: A second species, Alpine Musk Deer (Moschus sifanicus), is also recognised as occurring in the Himalaya. Not featured in this book.

65. INDIAN MUNTJAC (BARKING DEER)
(Plate 8)
Muntiacus muntjac

Identification: Shoulder height 50-75 cm. Chestnut to dark brown. Hind limbs longer than fore. Males have short antlers (5-8 cm) with a short brow tine, set on hairy pedicels (8-10 cm). Long upper canines.
Habitat: Dense forests, up to 2,400 metres elevation in the Himalaya.
Range: India, Nepal, Bhutan, Bangladesh, Sri Lanka and Pakistan.
Behaviour: Diurnal. Shy, venturing into open meadows from the jungle only for short periods to feed. Numbers usually seen together, 1-3. Distinctive shrill dog-like barks (hence Barking Deer); also makes a rattling noise when fleeing.
Diet: Leaves, grasses and fruit.
Breeding: Gestation 6 months. 1-2 young born at a time.
Status: Common. Especially in protected areas and suitable habitats.
Similar species: Hog Deer. Musk Deer.

66. CHITAL (SPOTTED DEER) *(Plate 8)*
Cervus axis

Identification: Shoulder height 70-90 cm. Yellow, light or dark brown upperparts with distinctive white spots; whitish underparts. Males with large antlers with 3 tines each - a brow tine and a forked main beam.
Habitat: Forests and grasslands, near water. Prefers unbroken plains.
Range: India, Nepal, Bhutan, Bangladesh, Sri Lanka and Pakistan. South of the Himalayan foothills.
Behaviour: Diurnal and nocturnal. Generally shy, but will enter cultivation near villages. Gregarious, often in groups of 20-50 animals, especially in open meadows. Large all-male herds can be seen. In forests frequently associates with troops of Hanuman Langur who drop tidbits from the treetops. Alarm call a loud whistle - "wow".
Diet: Grasses, leaves, flowers and fruit.
Breeding: Gestation 7 months. 1 young born at a time.
Status: Abundant. Especially in protected areas and forests.
Similar species: Hog Deer.

67. SWAMP DEER (BARASINGHA) *(Plate 8)*
Cervus duvauceli

Identification: Shoulder height 115-135 cm. Light or dark brown, yellowish brown or grey. Stags with a ruff and fine antlers, each with 12 or so points, hence the local name Barasingha (bara = 12, singha = horns, tines or antlers).
Habitat: Grasslands and forests, near marshes and swamps.
Range: Isolated pockets in N, C and NE India, to the south of the Himalayan foothills. Also SW Nepal.
Behaviour: Mainly nocturnal, but active during the mornings and evenings. Gregarious, with herds of up to 50 or more animals. Large all-male herds often seen. Shrill bays when alarmed, also emitted when on the run. Impressive bugling during the rut.
Diet: Grasses, leaves, flowers and fruit.
Breeding: Gestation 6 months. 1 young born at a time.
Status: Endangered. Isolated populations survive in a few protected areas.
Similar species: Red Deer. Thamin. Sambar.

---

68. RED DEER (KASHMIR STAG OR HANGUL)
(Plate 8)
Cervus elaphus

Identification: Shoulder height 120-150 cm. Light brown, rufous-grey or dark brown, with luxuriant winter coat. Large spreading antlers, each with 5 or more points.
Habitat: Forests and meadows, between 1,500 and 3,600 metres elevation.
Range: Kashmir (Dachigam), Himachal Pradesh (Gamagul) and Northern Bhutan.
Behaviour: Nocturnal and diurnal. Group size 2-18 animals, forming large assemblies during the winter at lower elevations. Altitudinal migration in search of food. Roars.
Diet: Grasses, leaves, flowers and fruit.
Breeding: Gestation 8 months. 1 young born at a time.
Status: Endangered.
Similar species: Swamp Deer. Thamin. Sambar.

---

69. THAMIN (MANIPUR BROW-ANTLERED DEER) *(Plate 8)*
Cervus eldii

Identification: Shoulder height 105-120 cm. Light fawn to dark brown, sometimes blackish; lighter during the summer. Large antlers, each with 6 points or tines, occasionally more, the main beam extending into the long brow tine in a continuous curve. Splayed hooves and elongated dew claws enable it to walk on soft "floating" swampy habitat.
Habitat: Grasslands, floating swamps or "phumdis" and riverine forests.
Range: Keibul Lamjao on the banks of the Logtak Lake in Manipur (NE India).
Behaviour: Mainly nocturnal. Gregarious, found in small groups.

Diet: Grasses, leaves and agricultural crops.
Breeding: Gestation 239-256 days. Usually 1 young born at a time.
Status: Endangered. Estimated population approximately 100. Threatened by habitat loss and hunting.
Similar species: Swamp Deer. Red Deer. Sambar.

70. HOG DEER *(Plate 8)*
Cervus porcinus

Identification: Shoulder height 66-74 cm. Light to dark brown. Develops white spots during the summer. Thick-set with relatively short limbs. Hog-like habit of crashing through the vegetation. Antlers usually 30 cm or less, each with 3 tines. Brow tine forms an acute angle to the main beam.
Habitat: Grasslands and riverine forests.
Range: North India, Nepal, Bhutan, Bangladesh, Sri Lanka (introduced) and Pakistan.
Behaviour: Nocturnal and diurnal. Shy. Seen singly or in small groups. In open grasslands 10 or more animals may gather in a loose group. Alarm call a whistle.
Diet: Grasses and leaves.
Breeding: Gestation 8 months. 1-2 young born at a time.
Status: Uncommon. Possibly vulnerable due to its specialised habitat.
Similar species: Chital.

71. SAMBAR *(Plate 8)*
Cervus unicolor

RANDY

Identification: Shoulder height 140-150 cm. Largest deer in the subcontinent. Light to dark brown, even blackish. Coarse coat, males with ruff. Large sturdy antlers each with 3 tines, rarely more.
Habitat: Forests, including hills, riverine forests and grasslands.
Range: India, Nepal, Bhutan, Bangladesh and Sri Lanka.
Behaviour: Nocturnal and diurnal. Shy. Normally seen in small herds of 4-20 animals. Alarm call a loud explosive "dhank" usually given on sighting Tiger or Leopard. Partial to water and will bath and feed in lakes, rivers and marshes.
Diet: Grasses, leaves, flowers and fruit.
Breeding: Gestation 8 months. 1-2 young born at a time.
Status: Abundant. Good populations in forests and protected areas.
Similar species: Swamp Deer. Red Deer. Thamin.

72. NILGAI *(Plate 9)*
Boselaphus tragocamelus

RANDY

Identification: Shoulder height 120-150 cm. Robust, with rump lower than withers. Young and females tawny, adult males metallic blue-grey. Both sexes have a dark dorsal fringe on their thick necks as well as a throat tuft, which is longer in males. Males have 15-20 cm horns.

Habitat: Forest, scrub and near cultivation. Prefers open areas.
Range: India, from the Himalayan foothills to Karnataka in the south, SW Nepal and Pakistan.
Behaviour: Diurnal and nocturnal. Shy. Seen in herds of 4-10 animals. Adult males solitary or form all-male herds. Grunts when alarmed. Habitually defecates at the same spots.
Diet: Grasses, leaves, flowers, fruit and crops.
Breeding: Gestation 8-9 months. 1 young born at a time.
Status: Abundant. Hindus regard the Nilgai as sacred, as it is considered to be related to Domestic Cattle (nil = blue, gai = cow). In some areas Nilgai is a pest.
Similar species: None.

73. FOUR-HORNED ANTELOPE (CHOWSINGHA)
(Plate 9)
Tetracerus quadricornis

Identification: Shoulder height 55-65 cm. Yellowish to reddish brown upperparts, whitish underparts. Dark stripes in front of limbs. Males have 2 pairs of horns, the front pair 1-3 cm, and the hind pair 8-10 cm.
Habitat: Open hill forests, grasslands and woodlands.
Range: Sub-Himalayan India and C Nepal.
Behaviour: Mainly nocturnal. Shy. Numbers seen together 1-6, usually near a source of water. Barks (like Indian Muntjac) and whistles.
Diet: Grasses and leaves.
Breeding: Gestation 8 months. 1-2 young born at a time.
Status: Uncommon.
Similar species: None.

74. CHIRU (TIBETAN ANTELOPE) *(Plate 9)*
Pantholops hodgsoni

Identification: Shoulder height 80 cm. Woolly coat, light yellowish brown upperparts, white underparts. Males with long (60-65 cm) horns, ringed in the front, gently diverging upwards and slightly forwards. Black or brown face and stripes in the front of limbs. Swollen muzzles. Females are hornless.
Habitat: Steppe grasslands of the transhimalayan deserts between 3,600 and 5,500 metres elevation.
Range: Northern Ladakh (India).
Behaviour: Crepuscular. Shy. Digs shallow depressions on the ground with hooves to lie up in. Numbers usually seen together, 1-4. Altitudinal movement according to the seasons and availability of food. Keeps to flat and open valleys near streams and rivers.
Diet: Grasses.
Breeding: 1 young born at a time.
Status: Endangered. Only small numbers visit the Chang Chen Mo Valley in Ladakh from across the Tibetan Plateau over the Lanak La pass. Hunted for its flesh, skin, and horns. Its soft underfur, called "pashm", is used for making the prized "shahtoos" shawls.
Similar species: None.

75. WATER BUFFALO *(Plate 9)*
Bubalus arnee

Identification: Shoulder height 155-180 cm. More robust version of the Domestic Buffalo. Black, with dirty white lower limbs. Large, flat, sweeping horns (triangular in cross-section), larger in males.
Habitat: Riverine forests, grasslands, marshes and near cultivation.
Range: SE Nepal, S Bhutan, and NE and Central India. Introduced to Sri Lanka.
Behaviour: Nocturnal and diurnal. Numbers seen together, 1-20 or more. Partial to water. Snorts, grunts and bellows. Cow with newborn calf can be aggressive.
Diet: Grasses, leaves and agricultural crops.
Breeding: Gestation 10 months. 1 young born at a time.
Status: Endangered. Population estimated at fewer than 1,000.
Similar species: Domestic Buffalo (to whom it is ancestral and with whom it readily inter-breeds). Not featured in this book.

76. GAUR (INDIAN BISON) *(Plate 9)*
Bos gaurus

Identification: Shoulder height 165-195 cm. World's largest bovine. Young males and females reddish brown, adult males shiny black; yellowish or white lower limbs. Whitish forehead, sweeping, pointed horns, larger in males. Dorsal ridge and dewlap, both more pronounced in males.
Habitat: Hill forests up to 1,800 metres elevation, occasionally in lowland grasslands and open meadows.
Range: N, NE and S India, Nepal and Bhutan.
Behaviour: Nocturnal and diurnal. Shy and avoids human settlements. Gregarious, with herd sizes of 5-30 or more animals. Grunts, snorts and bellows.
Diet: Grasses, leaves and tree barks. Regularly visits salt licks.
Breeding: Gestation 270-280 days. 1 young born at a time. Longevity 24 years.
Status: Vulnerable. Large herds in S and NE India, especially in national parks. Threatened by loss of habitat and diseases transmitted by domestic cattle. Estimated population 5,000.
Similar species: Mithun or Gayal (Bos frontalis), of whom the Gaur is an ancestor, through interbreeding with the Domestic Cow (Bos taurus). Neither species is featured in this book.

77. YAK *(Plate 9)*
Bos mutus

Identification: Shoulder height 160-180 cm. Blackish brown, with whitish muzzle. Long shaggy hair over most of the body. Long spreading horns. Thick set with a humped shoulder, short sturdy limbs, long tail, the distal half being very bushy and tufted.
Habitat: Mountain grasslands at between 4,000 and 6,000 metres elevation.
Range: N Ladakh, northern edge of the Himalaya adjoining the Tibetan Plateau, in N Kumaon, Nepal, Sikkim and Bhutan.

Behaviour: Shy. Gregarious, in groups of 10-20 or more animals, forming large gatherings during the spring. Altitudinal migration in search of food.
Diet: Grasses and shrubs. Snow (for water) and rock salts.
Breeding: Gestation 9 months. Usually 1 young born at a time . Interbreeds with the Domestic Cattle (Bos taurus).
Status: Vulnerable/endangered. Hunted for flesh, skin and fur.
Similar species: Domestic Yak (Bos grunniens) to whom it is ancestral. Domestic Yak is found in the Himalayan regions of India, Nepal and Bhutan and are particularly common in Arunachal Pradesh (NE India). Not featured in this book.

78. BLACKBUCK *(Plate 9)*
Antilope cervicapra

Identification: Shoulder height 70-80 cm. Young males and females with yellowish fawn upperparts, replaced by dark brown or jet black in adult males; white underparts. Adult males have 45-60 cm long spiral horns; females have none.
Habitat: Grasslands, near forests, open scrub and cultivation. Avoids thick forests and hills.
Range: India and Nepal.
Behaviour: Mainly diurnal. Shy. Gregarious, often seen in groups of 10-50 or more animals. Elegant in flight. During the rut the dominant males challenge others with low grunts and may control up to 50 or more females. Outside the rut the males live separate from females.
Diet: Grasses, leaves, crops and fruit.
Breeding: Gestation 6 months. 1-2 young born at a time. Longevity 12 years.
Status: Vulnerable. Declining populations because of hunting and habitat loss. Common in areas where it is protected due to religious sentiment by the Vishnois in Rajasthan and Haryana and by the Balagiriasis in Gujarat.
Similar species: Indian Gazelle.

79. INDIAN GAZELLE (CHINKARA) *(Plate 9)*
Gazella bennettii

Identification: Shoulder height 60-65 cm. Light chestnut upperparts, white underparts, long slender limbs. Horns of males closely-ringed, slender, S-shaped when viewed from the side, 25-30 cm long. Female horns 10-13 cm, without rings; some females hornless.
Habitat: Arid scrub, sparse forests, deserts and broken terrain up to 1,200 metres elevation.
Range: NW and C India, and Pakistan.
Behaviour: Nocturnal and diurnal. Shy. Group sizes of 2-30 or more animals. Can survive without water for long periods. Makes sneezing sounds "ha-chhi-phus".
Diet: Grasses, leaves, crops and fruit (eg pumpkins and melons).
Breeding: Gestation 5.5 months. 1-2 young born at a time.
Status: Vulnerable. Hunted for food and hide. Protected due to religious sentiment in Rajasthan and Gujarat (where good populations are found).
Similar species: Blackbuck.

80. COMMON GORAL *(Plate 10)*
Nemorhaedus goral

Identification: Shoulder height 65-70 cm. Goat-like. Grey or reddish brown mixed with black. Backward-curving, gently divergent, ringed horns (10-13 cm). Both sexes have horns.
Habitat: Hill forests and grasslands between 900 and 4,000 metres elevation.
Range: W, C and E Himalaya.
Behaviour: Diurnal. Normally seen in small groups of up to 10 individuals. Old males are solitary. Makes loud hisses.
Diet: Grasses and leaves.
Breeding: Gestation 250-260 days. 1 young born at a time.
Status: Insufficiently known. Presumed uncommon. Threatened by hunting.
Similar species: Mainland Serow.

81. MAINLAND SEROW *(Plate 10)*
Capricornis sumatraensis

Identification: Shoulder height 90-110 cm. Reddish to grey to black. Sturdy. Large head and ears; thick neck; short limbs, lower half whitish. Black horns 15-25 cm long. Regarded as intermediate between goats and antelopes.
Habitat: Hill and mountain forests between 800 and 3,000 metres elevation.
Range: W, C and E Himalaya.
Behaviour: Diurnal and nocturnal. Shy. Sure-footed in steep, broken terrain. Numbers seen together, 1-5. Whistling screams and snorts.
Diet: Grasses and leaves.
Breeding: Gestation 7-8 months. 1-2 young born at a time. Longevity 10 years.
Status: Endangered. Hunted for food and medicinal properties.
Similar species: Common Goral.

82. TAKIN *(Plate 10)*
Budorcas taxicolor

Identification: Shoulder height 100-110 cm. Golden yellow, dark brown or greyish black, usually with a dark dorsal stripe. Withers higher than rump. Sturdy body, short thick limbs, thick neck, large head and swollen muzzle. Short, compact horns (similar to those of the African Gnu), long woolly coat.
Habitat: Hill and mountain forests between 900 and 3,000 metres elevation, usually with bamboo and rhododendron.
Range: Bhutan and E Himalaya (NE India).
Behaviour: Gregarious, seen in groups of 10-20 or more animals, forming large assemblies in the summer. In the Jorging valley of Siang in Arunachal Pradesh (NE India) up to 300 animals are known to gather at hot sulphur springs. Altitudinal migration in search of food.
Diet: Grasses and leaves.
Breeding: 1 young born at a time.
Status: Uncommon. In Arunachal Pradesh hunted for skin, flesh and trophy. National

animal of Bhutan.
Similar species: None.

---

83. NILGIRI TAHR *(Plate 10)*
Hemitragus hylocrius

Identification: Shoulder height 100-110 cm. Upperparts of females and young grey or yellowish, of adult males dark brown or blackish, with a distinctive light patch (appears white from a distance) on the back. Underparts paler. Short wrinkled horns, up to 45 cm in males, shorter in females.
Habitat: Hill grasslands and edge of forests between 1,200 and 2,600 metres elevation. Partial to rocky terrain.
Range: Nilgiris, Anaimalais and adjoining hills of S India.
Behaviour: Active in early mornings and late afternoons and evenings. Shy. Seen in groups of 5-50 animals. Surefooted and alert.
Diet: Grasses and leaves.
Breeding: Gestation 6 months. 1-2 young born at a time. Longevity 16-18 years.
Status: Vulnerable. Estimated population 2,000+. The flesh is regarded as having medicinal value.
Similar species: Himalayan Tahr.

---

84. HIMALAYAN TAHR *(Plate 10)*
Hemitragus jemlahicus

Identification: Shoulder height 85-105 cm. Reddish brown. Adult males darker brown than females and young. Long hair on body, forming a conspicuous lighter coloured mane on neck and shoulders reaching down to the knees. Regarded as intermediate between goat-antelopes and goats
Habitat: Mountain forests and open terrain between 3,000 and 5,300 metres elevation.
Range: W, C and E Himalaya, from Pir Panjal to Bhutan.
Behaviour: Sure-footed in precipitous terrain. Gregarious, usually seen in herds of 5-10 or more animals. Shy, retreating to remote shelters and forest patches during the day.
Diet: Grasses and leaves.
Breeding: Gestation 6.5 months. 1 young born at a time.
Status: Vulnerable/endangered. Reasonable numbers in protected and inaccessible areas.
Similar species: Nilgiri Tahr.

---

85. WILD GOAT *(Plate 10)*
Capra aegagrus

Identification: Shoulder height 85-95 cm. Brownish grey, yellowish or reddish brown upperparts, whitish underparts. Males with dark beard on chin and scimitar shaped horns with undulating keel in front.
Habitat: Arid mountains, usually between 1,200 and 2,200 metres

41

elevation.
Range: Baluchistan and W Sind, in Pakistan.
Behaviour: Diurnal. Gregarious. Seen in herds of 6-20 or more animals. During the day retreats to the remotest parts of its range. Bleats (generally silent though).
Diet: Grasses and leaves.
Breeding: Gestation 22 weeks. 1 litter a year. 1-2 young born at a time. Longevity up to 20 years. Ancestor of the Domestic Goat (Capra hircus).
Status: Vulnerable. Declining numbers. The bezoar stone found in its stomach was valued as medicine in the Far East and in Europe.
Similar species: Ibex.

86. MARKHOR *(Plate 10)*
Capra falconeri

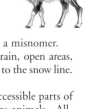

Identification: Shoulder height 80-100 cm. Distinctive straight spiralled horns up to 100 cm or longer. Females dark fawn. Males generally metallic grey mixed with brown and red. Old males mostly whitish, with a flowing mane and dark upper limbs. Dark beard, dorsal stripe and tail. Markhor in Persian means "snake eater", but this may be a misnomer.
Habitat: Diverse, exposed to fierce heat and cold. Rocky precipitous terrain, open areas, grassy glades and mountain forests, from 1,800 to 3,600 metres elevation up to the snow line.
Range: West of Kashmir, in W Himalaya, and Hindu Kush.
Behaviour: Crepuscular. During the middle of the day retreats into inaccessible parts of its home. Shy. Gregarious. Often seen in small groups of 5-10 or more animals. All-male groups are also seen.
Diet: Grasses, leaves and acorns.
Breeding: Gestation 5.5 months. 1-2 young born at a time.
Status: Endangered. Estimated world population 2,500.
Similar species: None.

87. IBEX *(Plate 10)*
Capra ibex

Identification: Shoulder height up to 100 cm. Colour variable - yellowish white tinged with brown and grey in the winter, brown mixed with white in the summer. Males have long scimitar-shaped horns (100 cm or more) with knobbed ridges in the front. Dark dorsal stripe from shoulders to the tail.
Habitat: Precipitous mountain terrain, between 3,650 and 6700 metres elevation, usually above the tree line.
Range: W Himalaya and N Pakistan.
Behaviour: Active early mornings and evenings. Gregarious, in herds of 5-50 animals or more. All male herds of 1-4 are also found. Retreats to remote spots when resting. Shrill whistles (alarm call). Altitudinal migration in search of food.
Diet: Grass and leaves.
Breeding: Gestation 5.5 months. 1 litter a year. 1-2 young born at a time. Longevity 12-15 years.
Status: Endangered. Hunted for its soft and luxurious under-fur, called "pashm", used

for making prized shawls.
Similar species: Wild Goat.

88. BHARAL (BLUE SHEEP) *(Plate 10)*
Pseudois nayaur

Identification: Shoulder height 90 cm. Brownish grey tinged with blue. Adult males have black stripes on the front of limbs and along the middle of the flanks. Older males have black on chest and face. Large sturdy horns 60 cm long. Shares characteristics of both sheep and goats.
Habitat: Open mountain steppe between the tree and the snow lines, between 4,000 and 6,500 metres elevation. Avoids forests and scrub.
Range: W, C and E Himalaya.
Behaviour: Mainly diurnal. Gregarious, seen in herds of 10-20 or more animals. Males form separate herds outside the rut. Their coats blend well with the dark rocks. Agile goat-like climber in precipitous country.
Diet: Grasses, leaves, mosses and lichens.
Breeding: Gestation 160 days. 1-2 young born at a time. Longevity 9-24 years.
Status: Vulnerable. Found mainly in protected areas and remote mountains.
Similar species: None.

89. INDIAN PANGOLIN *(Plate 11)*
Manis crassicaudata

Identification: Head and body 45-75 cm. Tail 33-45 cm. Upperparts, outside of limbs and tail armoured in large overlapping plates. 11-13 rows of body scales. Sparse bristly hair on underparts and in between plates.
Habitat: Forests and arid scrub.
Range: India, Nepal, Sri Lanka and Pakistan.
Behaviour: Nocturnal and shy. Terrestrial, but good tree climbers, assisted by their prehensile tails. Digs the earth for food with strong claws on the forefoot. Feeds with its long sticky tongue. Curls up into a ball in defence. Den a burrow. Mother carries young on tail. Hisses.
Diet: Ants, termites, their eggs, insects and grubs.
Breeding: 1-2 young born at a time. Longevity 13 years.
Status: Vulnerable. Hunted for its alleged superstitious and medicinal value.
Similar species: Chinese Pangolin (Manis pentadactyla). Not featured in this book.

90. INDIAN PALM SQUIRREL *(Plate 11)*
Funambulus palmarum

Identification: Head and body 13-15 cm. Tail 14-16 cm. Light to dark greyish brown upperparts with three pale dorsal stripes; underparts pale. Bushy tail peppered with black and white.
Habitat: Forests and scrubs.

43

Range: S India and Sri Lanka.
Behaviour: Diurnal. Not shy. Arboreal and terrestrial. Numbers usually seen 2-7. Shrill repetitive bird-like chirruping calls. Den a hole in tree or wall, or under the roofs of houses.
Diet: Shoots, buds, flowers, nectar, fruit, barks, birds' eggs and insects.
Breeding: Gestation 6 weeks. 2-3 young born at a time.
Status: Abundant.
Similar species: Northern Palm Squirrel.

---

91. NORTHERN PALM SQUIRREL *(Plate 11)*
Funambulus pennantii

Identification: Head and body 13-15 cm. Tail 14-16 cm. Greyish brown upperparts with 5 pale dorsal stripes. Bushy tail peppered with white and black.
Habitat: Gardens, woodlands, parks, villages, cities and urban areas.
Range: N India, Nepal, Bhutan, Bangladesh, Sri Lanka and Pakistan.
Behaviour: Diurnal. Not shy near human settlements. Seen in small groups of 3-10 animals. Makes shrill bird-like calls.
Diet: Shoots, buds, flowers, fruit, barks and birds' eggs.
Breeding: Gestation 6 weeks. 2-3 young born at a time.
Status: Abundant.
Similar species: Indian Palm Squirrel.

---

92. BLACK GIANT SQUIRREL *(Plate 11)*
Ratufa bicolor

Identification: Head and body 35-40 cm. Tail 60 cm. Dark brown to blackish upperparts, buff underparts.
Habitat: Forests.
Range: E Nepal, Bhutan and NE India.
Behaviour: Active in the mornings and evenings. Shy and difficult to see. Seen singly or in pairs. Largely arboreal, leaps in the tree tops, from branch to branch and tree to tree. Den a nest of leaves and twigs on branches of trees. Makes loud rattling calls.
Diet: Fruit, barks, insects and larvae.
Breeding: Gestation 28 days. 1-2 young born at a time.
Status: Insufficiently known. Probably common.
Similar species: Indian Giant Squirrel.

---

93. INDIAN GIANT SQUIRREL
(Plate 11)
Ratufa indica

Identification: Head and body 35-40 cm. Tail 60 cm. Blackish upperparts, with red head and flanks, whitish underparts.
Habitat: Deciduous and moist evergreen forests.

Range: S and C India.
Behaviour: Diurnal. Mainly crepuscular. Shy. Agile. Territorial. Mainly arboreal, moving between trees with ease. Den several globular nests of leaves and twigs in treetops. Makes loud rattles and scolds, when alarmed. Rests on its belly draped over the curve of a branch.
Diet: Fruit, flowers and barks.
Breeding: Presumed similar to the Black Giant Squirrel.
Status: Endangered. Hunted for its flesh.
Similar species: Black Giant Squirrel.

94. GRIZZLED INDIAN SQUIRREL *(Plate 11)*
Ratufa macroura

Identification: Head and Body 28-41 cm. Tail 31-41 cm. Upperparts grey or brownish grey, grizzled with white, head blackish; underparts lighter.
Habitat: Forests, including hills, between 200 and 2,300 metres elevation.
Range: Localised areas in S India and Sri Lanka.
Behaviour: Crepuscular. Shy. Arboreal. Jumps from one tree to another with ease. Den a nest of twigs in branches.
Diet: Fruit, barks, leaves, shoots, rarely birds' eggs and insects.
Breeding: Gestation 28 days. 1-2 young born at a time.
Status: Endangered. Estimated world population 300, due to loss of habitat. Srivilipultur and Chinnar sanctuaries in S India especially set aside for its protection.
Similar species: None.

95. ORANGE-BELLIED HIMALAYAN SQUIRREL *(Plate 11)*
Dremomys lokriah

Identification: Head and body 20 cm. Tail 22 cm. Reddish brown upperparts; orange throat, chest and belly.
Habitat: Forests, up to 2,700 metres elevation.
Range: Nepal, Bhutan and NE India.
Behaviour: Diurnal. Shy. Feeds in trees and on the ground. Den a hole in a tree or a nest in branches. Makes loud cackles.
Diet: Fruit and nuts.
Breeding: Not much is known of its breeding habits.
Status: Insufficiently known. Probably common.
Similar species: Irrawaddy Squirrel or Hoary-bellied Himalayan Squirrel (Callosciurus pygerythrus). Not featured in this book.

malabar squirrel - TREE HOUSE

55

96. LONG-TAILED MARMOT *(Plate 11)*
Marmota caudata

Identification: Head and body 60 cm. Tail 30-35 cm. Rich tawny, orange or red; black back, also on crown and tail.
Habitat: Montane forests and alpine pastures from 2,400 to 4,300 metres elevation.
Range: Kashmir (N India) and N Pakistan.
Behaviour: Diurnal. Gregarious. Lives in large colonies in burrows up to 5-7 metres deep. Sits upright to get a better view. Hibernates during the winter. Shy. Makes shrill whistling screams when alarmed.
Diet: Grasses, leaves, flowers, fruit, seeds and roots.
Breeding: Gestation 30-35 days. 2-4 young born at a time.
Status: Insufficiently known. Probably common.
Similar species: Himalayan Marmot.

---

97. HIMALAYAN MARMOT *(Plate 11)*
Marmota himalayana

Identification: Head and body 60 cm. Tail 13 cm. Tawny, with black on upperparts. Dark face and tail tip.
Habitat: Mountain terrain from 4,000 to 5,500 metres elevation.
Range: W and C Himalaya.
Behaviour: Diurnal. Shy. Gregarious, lives in large colonies in extensive burrows. Makes shrill calls. Hibernates during the winter.
Diet: Leaves, grasses, flowers, fruit, nuts and roots.
Breeding: 2-4 young born at a time.
Status: Insufficiently known. Probably common.
Similar species: Long-tailed marmot.

---

98. RED GIANT FLYING SQUIRREL *(Plate 12)*
Petaurista petaurista

Identification: Head and body 45 cm. Tail 60 cm. Red or chestnut upperparts, pale underparts. Large, dark, protuberant eyes for night vision.
Habitat: Deciduous to evergreen forests.
Range: W, C and E Himalaya, up to the tree line.
Behaviour: Nocturnal. Shy. Den a hole in tree. Glides from tree to tree with its extended parachute-like membrane between limbs. Sociable, attracts others with loud calls.
Diet: Fruit, nuts, bark, resins, insects and larvae.
Breeding: 1-2 young born at a time.
Status: Insufficiently known. Hunted by tribal peoples.
Similar species: Spotted Giant Flying Squirrel. Not featured in this book.

99. PARTICOLOURED FLYING SQUIRREL
(Plate 12)
Hylopetes alboniger

Type: Flying squirrel.
Identification: Head and body 25-30 cm. Tail 25-30 cm. Hoary or black upperparts, white underparts.
Habitat: Forests, from 1,800 metres elevation up to the tree line.
Range: Nepal, Bhutan and NE India.
Behaviour: Nocturnal. Shy.
Diet: Shoots, buds and leaves.
Breeding: Not much is known about its breeding habits.
Status: Insufficiently known.
Similar species: Kashmir Pygmy Flying Squirrel.

100. KASHMIR PYGMY FLYING SQUIRREL
(Plate 12)
Hylopetes fimbriatus

Identification: Head and body 25-30 cm. Tail 25-30 cm. Reddish brown mixed with black upperparts, pale underparts.
Habitat: Forests above 1,800 metres elevation.
Range: N India (Jammu and Kashmir and Himachal Pradesh) and N Pakistan.
Behaviour: Nocturnal. Shy. Glides from tree to tree. Den a nest in trees.
Diet: Buds, shoots, fruit and nuts.
Breeding: Not much is known about its breeding habits.
Status: Insufficiently known.
Similar species: Particoloured Flying Squirrel.

101. HODGSON'S SHORT-TAILED PORCUPINE *(Plate 12)*
Hystrix brachyura

Identification: Head and body 70-90 cm. Short tail. Chunky animal with sharp spines on the body and hollow ended spines on the tail. Dorsal mane, when present, up to 15 cm.
Habitat: Forests and grasslands up to 1,500 metres elevation.
Range: E Nepal, Bhutan, Bangladesh and NE India.
Behaviour: Shy. Mainly nocturnal. Seen singly or in small family parties of 2-4 animals. Den a burrow in the ground or a shelter in thick vegetation.
Diet: Fruit, grains, roots and cultivation. Bones for minerals.
Breeding: Not much is known about its breeding habits.
Status: Insufficiently known. Presumably rare.
Similar species: Indian Porcupine.

102. INDIAN PORCUPINE *(Plate 12)*
Hystrix indica

Identification: Head and body 70-90 cm. Tail 8-10 cm. Dark, covered in long black or brown and white spines, with a distinctive dorsal crest 15-30 cm long.
Habitat: Forests, scrub and grasslands up to 2,400 metres elevation.
Range: India, Nepal, Bhutan, Bangladesh, Sri Lanka and Pakistan.
Behaviour: Mainly nocturnal. Shy. Numbers usually seen 1-4. Den a burrow in the ground, usually with more than one exit, often several metres long, ending in a spacious chamber. There are usually gnawed bones at the entrance. May fatally wound Tiger or Leopard with its long and sharp quills, delivered while rushing at its foe at speed in reverse. Does not shoot quills, as is often locally believed. Makes rattling noise with hollow tail quills.
Diet: Fruit, roots and crops. Bones for minerals.
Breeding: Gestation 240 days. 2-4 young born at a time.
Status: Common. Hunted for its flesh.
Similar species: Hodgson's Short-tailed Porcupine.

---

103. LARGE-EARED PIKA *(Plate 12)*
Ochotona macrotis

Identification: Head and body 15-20 cm. No tail or very short. Chubby. Rounded head with short muzzle and large rounded ears. Long dense hair on the inside of the ears. Brownish grey upperparts, with pale russet in the head and the front; underparts whitish. Although related to rabbits it look more like a rat.
Habitat: High mountains from 2,300 to 6,100 metres elevation. Rocky areas, alpine deserts, and spruce forests. Generally found at higher altitudes than the Royle's Pika.
Range: Karakoram (N Pakistan) and W and C Himalaya (east to Bhutan).
Behaviour: Mainly active during midday. Does not gather hay for the winter and cache food like other non-Himalayan Pikas. Makes sharp whistles, etc, but does not vocalise much.
Diet: Grasses, leaves, twigs, mosses and lichens.
Breeding: 2 or more litters per year. 1-6 young born at a time.
Status: Insufficiently known. Probably common.
Similar species: Royle's Pika (often regarded as the same species).

---

104. ROYLE'S PIKA *(Plate 12)*
Ochotona roylei

Identification: Head and body 15-20 cm. No tail or very short. Chubby. Rounded head with short muzzle and large rounded ears. Ears less wide than the Large-eared Pika's, and with shorter, less dense hairs on the insides. Dark grey rufous upperparts, with head, front and shoulders bright chestnut; white or greyish underparts.
Habitat: High mountains, rocky terrain, rhododendron and spruce forests, from 2,400 to 4,300 metres elevation. Occasionally in the rocky walls of houses. Usually occurs at lower elevations than the Large-eared Pika.

Range: Karakoram (N Pakistan) and W and C Himalaya (N India, east to Nepal).
Behaviour: Diurnal and crepuscular. Lives in family groups. Makes low calls and high-pitched whistles, etc. Occasionally known to make hay piles and cache food (the Large-eared Pika is said to display this behaviour to a lesser degree).
Diet: Grasses, leaves, lichens and mosses.
Breeding: 1-5 young born at a time.
Status: Insufficiently known. Probably common.
Similar species: Large-eared Pika (often regarded as the same species).

105. HISPID HARE *(Plate 12)*
Caprolagus hispidus

Identification: Head and body 40-50 cm. Tail 2.5-3 cm (all brown). Short ears 5-7 cm. Dark brown mixed with black coarse hair on upperparts, brownish white underparts.
Habitat: Grasslands at the edge of forests in the foothills of the "duns", "terai" and "duars".
Range: N and NE India (from Uttar Pradesh to Assam), Nepal, Bhutan and possibly Bangladesh.
Behaviour: More rabbit-like than hare. Small home ranges (2,800 sq metres for females and 8,200 sq metres for males). Numbers seen together, 1-3. Slow moving.
Diet: Grasses, leaves, shoots, barks and fruit.
Breeding: Litter size likely to be small as females appear to have 4 teats. 1 or more young born at a time.
Status: Endangered. Probably less rare than it is considered to be. Believed to be extinct until rediscovered recently. Threats from annual burning of its grassland habitat in many parts of its range.
Similar species: Indian Hare.

106. INDIAN HARE *(Plate 12)*
Lepus nigricollis

Identification: Head and body 40-50 cm. Tail 10 cm. Reddish brown upperparts mixed with black, white underparts, rufous tail. Some with black or grey nape. Long ears, hence Khargosh (khar = ass, and gosh = ears) in Persian and Hindustani.
Habitat: Forests, grasslands, including hills, up to 2,400 metres elevation, and cultivation.
Range: India, Nepal, Bhutan, Bangladesh, Sri Lanka and Pakistan.
Behaviour: Mainly nocturnal. Shy. Numbers usually seen 1-4. Home ranges up to 10 or more hectares. Den a "form" scraped on the ground with its paws.
Diet: Grasses, leaves, flowers, fruit and cultivation.
Breeding: 1-4 or more young born at a time.
Status: Abundant.
Similar species: Hispid Hare.

Spotted Linsang

Slow Loris (p 10)
Nycticebus coucang

Rhesus Macaque (p 10)
Macaca mulatta

Assam Macaque (p 10)
Macaca assamensis

Liontail Macaque (p 11)
Macaca silenus

♀

Bonnet Macaque
Macaca radiata
(p 11)
♂

Hoolock Gibbon
Hylobates hoolock
(p 12)

Hanuman Langur (p 12)
Presbytis entellus

Golden Leaf Monkey (p 13)
Presbytis geei

Nilgiri Langur (p 13)
Presbytis johnii

30 cm

Capped Leaf Monkey
Presbytis pileatus
(p 13)

PLATE 2

Golden Jackal (p 14)
Canis aureus

Wolf
Canis lupus (p 14)

Bengal Fox
Vulpes bengalensis
(p 15)

30 cm

Red Fox (p 15)
Vulpes vulpes

Dhole
Cuon alpinus (p 15)

Asiatic Black Bear (p 16)
Selenarctos thibetanus

Brown Bear
Ursus arctos
(p 16)

Red Panda (p 17)
Ailurus fulgens

60 cm

Sloth Bear (p 16)
Melursus ursinus

PLATE 3

Yellow-bellied Weasel
Mustela kathiah
(p 17)

10 cm

Himalayan Weasel
Mustela sibirica
(p18)

Mountain Weasel
Mustela altaica (p 18)

Yellow-throated Marten
Martes flavigula (p 18)

30 cm

Beech Marten
Martes foina (p 19)

Ratel
Mellivora capensis
(p 19)

Smooth-coated Otter (p 20)
Lutra perspicillata

Eurasian Otter (p 19)
Lutra lutra

Oriental Small-clawed Otter (p 20)
Aonyx cinerea

Small Indian Civet
Viverricula indica
(p 21)

Large Indian Civet (p 21)
Viverra zibetha

PLATE 4

Spotted Linsang (p 21)
Prionodon pardicolor

Three-striped Palm Civet
Arctogalidea trivirgata
(p 22)

Masked Palm Civet
Paguma larvata (p 22)

30 cm

Common Palm Civet
Paradoxurus hermaphroditus
(p 22)

Binturong
Arctictis binturong (p 23)

30 cm

Indian Grey Mongoose
Herpestes edwardsii
(p 23)

Small Indian Mongoose
Herpestes auropunctatus
(p 23)

Ruddy Mongoose
Herpestes smithii
(p 24)

Crab-eating Mongoose
Herpestes urva
(p 24)

Stripe-necked Mongoose
Herpestes vitticollis   (p 24)

PLATE 5

Striped Hyaena (p 24)
Hyaena hyaena

30 cm

Leopard Cat (p 25)
Felis bengalensis

Caracal (p 25)
Felis caracal

Jungle Cat (p 26)
Felis chaus

Marbled Cat (p 26)
Felis marmorata

Wild Cat (p 27)
Felis silvestris

Pallas's Cat (p 26)
Felis manul

Rusty-spotted Cat (p 27)
Felis rubiginosa

Asiatic Golden Cat (p 27)
Felis temminckii

Fishing Cat (p 28)
Felis viverrina

PLATE 6

Eurasian Lynx
Lynx lynx (p 28)

60 cm

♂

Lion
Panthera leo
(p 28)

♀

(black)

Leopard
Panthera pardus
(p 29)

(white)

Tiger (p 29)
Panthera tigris

Snow Leopard (p 30)
Panthera uncia

Clouded Leopard (p 30)
Neofelis nebulosa

PLATE 7

Ganges Dolphin (p 30)
Platanista gangetica

Indian Elephant
Elephas maximus
(p 31)

(Kutch)

Asiatic Wild Ass
Equus hemionus
(p 31)

(Ladakh)

Wild Boar (p 33)
Sus scrofa

60 cm

Indian Rhinoceros
Rhinoceros unicornis
(p 32)
120 cm

30 cm

Pygmy Hog
Sus salvanius (p 32)

Indian Spotted Chevrotain
Tragulus meminna (p 33)

PLATE 8

50 cm

Forest Musk Deer
Moschus chrysogaster
(p 33)

Indian Muntjac
Muntiacus muntjac (p 34)

Hog Deer
Cervus porcinus
(p 36)

Chital
Cervus axis
(p 34)

Swamp Deer
Cervus duvauceli
(p 35)

Red Deer (p 35)
Cervus elaphus

100 cm

Sambar (p 36)
Cervus unicolor

Thamin
Cervus eldii
(p 35)

PLATE 9

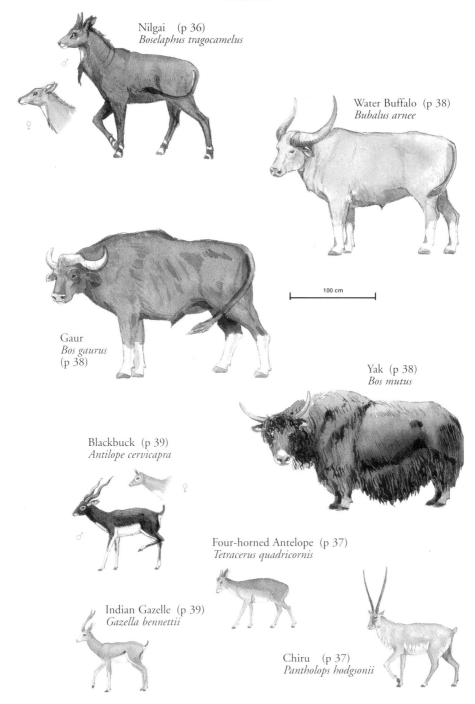

Nilgai (p 36)
Boselaphus tragocamelus

Water Buffalo (p 38)
Bubalus arnee

100 cm

Gaur
Bos gaurus
(p 38)

Yak (p 38)
Bos mutus

Blackbuck (p 39)
Antilope cervicapra

Four-horned Antelope (p 37)
Tetracerus quadricornis

Indian Gazelle (p 39)
Gazella bennettii

Chiru (p 37)
Pantholops hodgsonii

PLATE 10

Common Goral
Nemorhaedus goral
(p 40)

Mainland Serow (p 40)
Capricornis sumatraensis

Takin (p 40)
Budorcas taxicolor

Nilgiri Tahr
Hemitragus hylocrius
(p 41)

Markhor (p 42)
Capra falconeri

Himalayan Tahr (p 41)
Hemitragus jemlahicus

Wild Goat
Capra aegagrus
(p 41)

Ibex
Capra ibex (p 42)

Bharal
Pseudois nayaur
(p 43)

100 cm

Long-tailed Marmot
Marmota caudata
(p 46)

Indian Pangolin (p 43)
Manis crassicaudata

30 cm

Himalayan Marmot (p 46)
Marmota himalayana

Black Giant Squirrel (p 44)
Ratufa bicolor

Northern Palm Squirrel
Funambulus pennantii
(p 44)

Indian Giant Squirrel
Ratufa indica
(p 44)

Orange-bellied Himalayan Squirrel
Dremomys lokriah
(p 45)

Indian Palm Squirrel
Funambulus palmarum
(p 43)

15 cm

Grizzled Indian Squirrel
Ratufa macroura (p 45)

61

PLATE 12

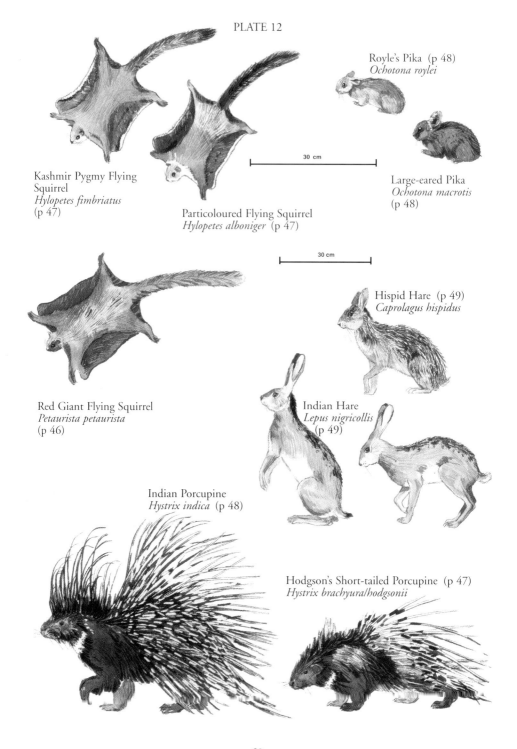

Royle's Pika (p 48)
Ochotona roylei

30 cm

Kashmir Pygmy Flying
Squirrel
Hylopetes fimbriatus
(p 47)

Large-eared Pika
Ochotona macrotis
(p 48)

Particoloured Flying Squirrel
Hylopetes alboniger (p 47)

30 cm

Hispid Hare (p 49)
Caprolagus hispidus

Red Giant Flying Squirrel
Petaurista petaurista
(p 46)

Indian Hare
Lepus nigricollis
(p 49)

Indian Porcupine
Hystrix indica (p 48)

Hodgson's Short-tailed Porcupine (p 47)
Hystrix brachyura/hodgsonii

62

PLATE 13

Rhesus Macaque
$^1/_2$ natural size

Fore foot

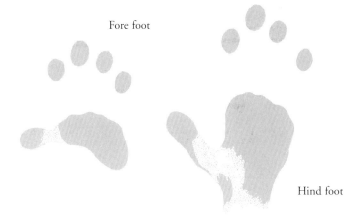

Hind foot

Hanuman Langur
$^1/_2$ natural size

Fore foot

Hind foot

PLATE 14

Golden Jackal
Natural size

Dhole
Natural size

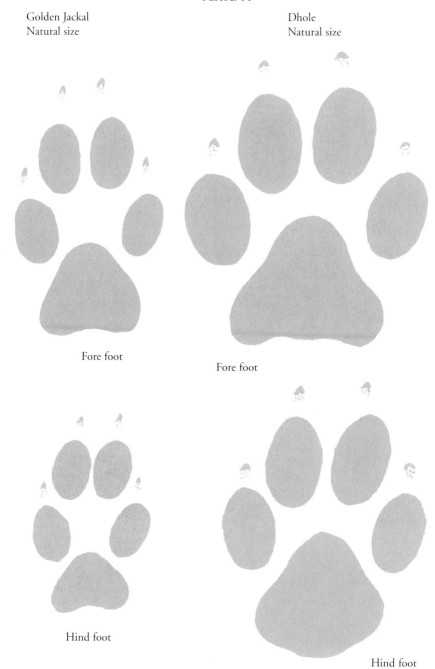

Fore foot

Fore foot

Hind foot

Hind foot

PLATE 15

Sloth Bear
$1/2$ natural size

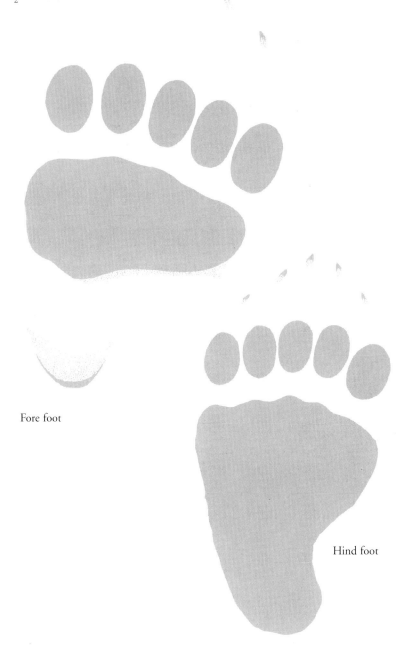

Fore foot

Hind foot

PLATE 16

Yellow-throated Marten
Natural size

Smooth-coated Otter
Natural size

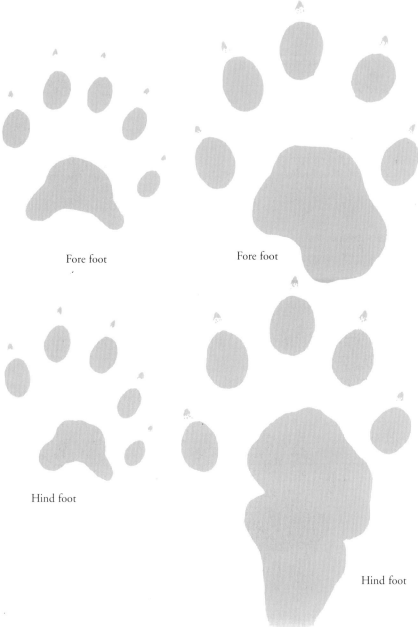

Fore foot

Fore foot

Hind foot

Hind foot

PLATE 17

Small Indian Civet
Natural size

Large Indian Civet
Natural size

Common Palm Civet
$^3/_4$ natural size

Crab-eating Mongoose
$^3/_4$ natural size

Fore foot

Fore foot

Hind foot

Hind foot

PLATE 18

Jungle Cat
$^3/_4$ natural size

Fishing Cat
$^3/_4$ natural size

Leopard
$^3/_4$ natural size

Fore foot

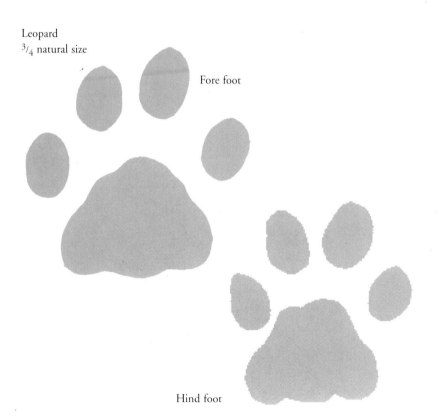

Hind foot

PLATE 19

Tiger
$^1/_2$ natural size

Fore foot

Hind foot

PLATE 20

Indian Rhinoceros
$^1/_3$ natural size

PLATE 21

Wild Boar
$^3/_4$ natural size

Chital
$^3/_4$natural size

Indian Muntjac
$^3/_4$ natural size

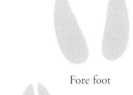

Fore foot

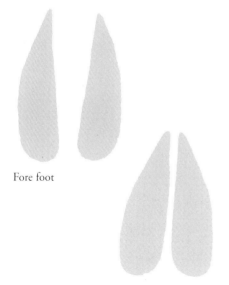

Fore foot

Hind foot

Hind foot

PLATE 22

Sambar
Natural size

Fore foot

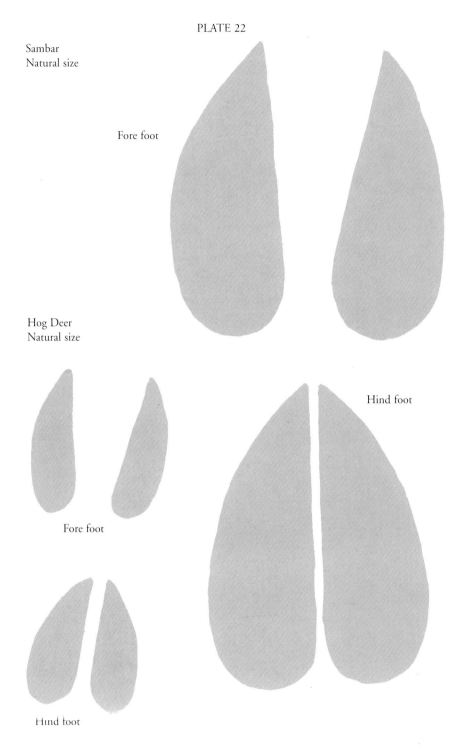

Hog Deer
Natural size

Hind foot

Fore foot

Hind foot

PLATE 23

Gaur
$1/2$ natural size

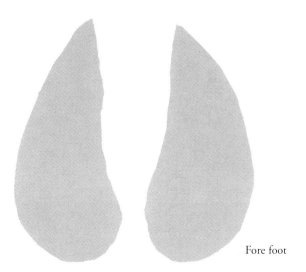

Fore foot

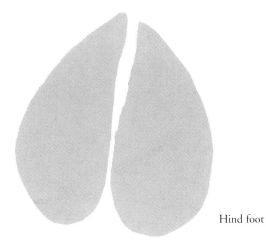

Hind foot

PLATE 24

Porcupine
$^3/_4$ natural size

Indian Hare
Natural size

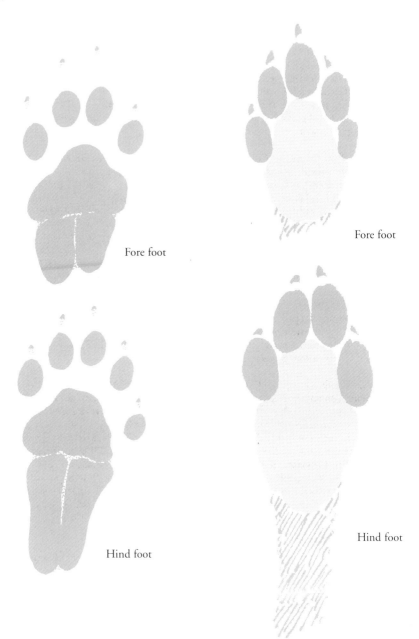

Fore foot

Fore foot

Hind foot

Hind foot

74

WHERE TO WATCH MAMMALS

The Indian subcontinent has a large number of national parks and many offer excellent opportunities for mammal-watching. In this section we have chosen only the better known national parks and our choice has been dictated by the following factors: they harbour good populations of mammals (particularly the larger species), they are different enough from other parks to make a visit there worthwhile, and, with a few exceptions, they are reasonably accessible and have a modicum of tourism infrastructure. Usually each of the national parks chosen has some large spectacular mammal as its star attraction. We have taken care to include national parks that are representative of the major habitat types found in the Indian subcontinent, with the exception of the desert.

It is possible to combine a visit to national parks with a cultural tour, taking in ancient cities, grand palaces and forts, archaeological sites, ornate temples, quaint hill stations, thriving bazaars, centuries-old fairs and festivals, and beach resorts, not to mention the diverse and colourful peoples that inhabit the land. Many of the national parks featured in this book are located near one or more cultural tourist attractions. For example, Chitwan near Kathmandu and Pokhara, Sariska and Bharatpur near Delhi, Agra and Jaipur, Bandhavgarh near Khajuraho, Nagarhole-Bandipur-Mudumalai near Bangalore, Mysore and Ooty, and Yala near Colombo.

Infrastructure for wildlife tourism within the subcontinent is still in the developing stage (although Nepal seems to be better developed than its neighbours). The Forest Lodges, run by the national or state governments, usually have good locations within the park and provide moderate/basic accommodation and adequate food. There are also Forest Rest Houses within the park, normally for use by the forest officials, which, if vacant, are available for tourists, but most of them do not have catering. There are also a number of private lodges and camps, usually at the park's edge, that provide accommodation and services aimed largely at foreign visitors.

Many national parks in the region offer elephant rides where visitors are taken out by a 'mahout' ('phanit' in Nepal) in search of wildlife. Riding elephants offer many advantages: they will go where other means of transport will not (eg the tangled elephant grass jungle, swamp or forest ravine), they allow you to observe large mammals at close range, they are extremely sure-footed in difficult terrain, and they are reliable and will hold their ground in front of large mammals like the Indian Rhinoceros, Tiger, Gaur, Wild Buffalo, or, indeed, the wild Indian Elephant. Riding elephants are not comfortable though, nor is it easy to take photographs from elephant back, but the experience is exciting and unique. Other means of transport in the subcontinent include 4-wheel drive motor vehicles, boats, and cycle rickshaws (in Keoladeo, Bharatpur). Most national parks have 'machans' or hides overlooking a body of water, meadow, or salt lick. Walking is prohibited in most non-Himalayan national parks, except in Nepal where walking is allowed in all parks.

For entry into a national park a valid permit is required, which can be obtained at the park headquarters (often some distance from the park itself). In Nepal entry permits may be obtained from selected guard posts at the park's edge on arrival. There are additional charges for still, cine and video photography, the amounts and rules varying from park to park and country to country. Flash photography is not allowed in many Indian parks. Separate, more stringent, rules apply for commercial photography and filming within national parks. Bring plenty of film, as it is not available inside the park or often even in nearby towns.

Safaris into many national parks are only allowed in the early mornings and the late afternoons, to coincide with the periods of productive mammal and wildlife watching. Generally a Forest Department guide will accompany each vehicle or group to identify the common animal species found in the park. In Nepal, safaris can be conducted at any time during the day, between sunrise and sunset. Night-time safaris with spotlights were stopped in the subcontinent many years ago.

If you have plenty of time, it is possible to organise your own wildlife safari by booking accommodation in advance and by using local transportation. However, often forest lodges and rest houses get booked up quickly during the season, due to the limited number of rooms, and it is possible that there will be no accommodation available when you arrive at the park, in spite of advance reservations. A 'do-it-yourself' mammal or wildlife tour of the subcontinent is only suitable for those who have no time restrictions.

For most people with limited time we strongly recommend that you use the services of a professional travel company either in your own country or in the subcontinent to organise your mammal-watching tour. The travel company will be able to advise you on the itinerary, depending on your interest and the time of year. They will be familiar with the national park rules and regulations, the best times to visit them, the best places to stay in relative to your budget, and the best means of transportation to and from the parks. This should leave you free fully to enjoy watching mammals, rather than spend valuable time making your own travel arrangements within the subcontinent which can be very time consuming.

The number of visitors to national parks in the subcontinent is on the increase. We hope that this book will help you to decide which national parks you wish to visit and will serve as a field guide to the mammals within them. From a long list we have agonised over which parks to include and which not to. The decision has not been easy. Our final list has 23 parks or park groups (in all there are 27 parks included). In our view they represent some of the finest national parks in the subcontinent.

NATIONAL PARK	COUNTRY	STAR ATTRACTIONS
Annapurna Conservation Area	Nepal	Red Panda, Blue Sheep
Bandhavgarh National Park	India	Tiger, Indian Gazelle
Bardia National Park	Nepal	Tiger, Swamp Deer
Chitwan National Park	Nepal	Indian Rhinoceros, Tiger
Corbett National Park	India	Tiger, Indian Elephant
Dachigam National Park	India	Red Deer, Asiatic Black Bear
Dudhwa National Park	India	Swamp Deer, Tiger
Gir National Park	India	Lion, Leopard
Hemis National Park	India	Snow Leopard, Bharal
Kanha National Park	India	Swamp Deer, Tiger
Kaziranga National Park	India	Rhinoceros, Wild Buffalo

Keoladeo Ghana or Bharatpur National Park	India	Mainly birds, Fishing Cat, Jungle Cat
Manas National Parks	India and Bhutan	Golden Langur, Wild Buffalo
Nagarhole-Bandipur-Mudumalai National Parks	India	Indian Elephant, Gaur, Dhole
Namdapha National Park	India	Clouded Leopard Hoolock Gibbon
Periyar National Park	India	Lion tail Macaque, Niligiri Langur
Ranthambhor National Park	India	Tiger, Caracal
Sagarmatha National Park	Nepal	Musk Deer, Himalayan Tahr
Sariska National Park	India	Indian Porcupine, Striped Hyaena
Sukla Phanta National Park	Nepal	Swamp Deer, Indian Elephant
Sunderbans National Parks	India and Bangladesh	Tiger, Spotted Deer Estuarine Crocodile
Yala/Ruhuna National Park	Sri Lanka	Indian Elephant, Sloth Bear
Wilpattu National Park	Sri Lanka	Leopard, Sloth Bear

DISCLAIMER

It should be stressed that while this section of the book has been written to provide practical advice on the various national parks, we take no responsibility should your experiences fall short of your expectations. We cannot guarantee that all or any of the mammals specified in each park will be seen during your visit, nor that you will be satisfied with the accommodation and the facilities. Management of parks, lodges and camps change, for better or worse. The parks face a constant threat from encroachment and poaching, and the time of year can make a big difference to the success of your visit.

Political turmoil in certain parts of the Indian subcontinent may make it inadvisable to visit national parks in those areas. Therefore, please check with your tour operator prior to your visit.

1. ANNAPURNA CONSERVATION AREA (NEPAL)

Area: 266,000 hectares.

Established: Proposed as a national park.

Description: The Annapurna Conservation Area in Central Nepal encloses the massive Annapurna Himalaya within its boundaries and is one the most spectacular landscapes on earth. The Kali Gandaki river, which flows along its western boundary, is the world's deepest gorge, lying 6,780 metres below the peaks of Annapurna I to the east and the Dhaulagiri range to the west. Another major attraction is the 'Annapurna sanctuary', a natural amphitheatre surrounded by seven peaks over 7,000 metres. The southern flanks of the park receive heavy rainfall during the monsoon, while the northern rainshadow areas receive little rain. There are tropical forests with Sal trees in the lower altitudes and temperate forests with Oak, Birch and Rhododendron higher up in the north. Above the tree line at 4,000 metres are alpine scrub and meadows. In the more remote areas, it is possible to see Musk Deer, Red Panda, Bharal and, if lucky, Snow Leopard. Because of its sheer altitudinal range, Annapurna is a haven for birdwatchers, with about 450 species known. The birds of the area include Lammergeier, Golden Eagle, Dark-breasted Rosefinch and Orange-rumped Honeyguide. All the six Himalayan pheasants are found here: Kalij, Cheer, Blood, Koklass, Satyr Tragopan and Himalayan Monal, Nepal's national bird.

Season: Open year-round, the best periods being October-November and March-April. There is heavy rainfall between June and September in the southern parts.

Access: Fly from Kathmandu to Pokhara (30 minutes) and drive to the beginning of your trekking trail. There are new motorable roads from Pokhara to the southern fringes of the park.

Accommodation and facilities: There are numerous 'tea houses' and tourist lodges along the popular trekking trails, but most tend to be basic (usually village homes with spare space for a few sleeping bags). A large proportion of visitors to Annapurna overnight in trekking tents, camping near villages or sources of running water. In the lower hills, not far from Pokhara, there are also some good purpose-built lodges, including Birethanti Lodge and Laxmi Lodge. Pokhara, the nearest town, has several hotels, ranging from budget to first class. The Fish Tail Lodge, on the banks of the Phewa Lake, is the oldest, and the Shangrila Village is a superb new resort. Annapurna has many excellent trekking trails and for mammal watching you are recommended to set aside more days for camping, especially along the less-frequented trails.

Note:

Annapurna has a permanent population of 40,000 inhabitants who live in settlements throughout the conservation area. Each year some 25,000 foreign trekkers also visit the park, some staying for up to 30 days or longer. Management is therefore aimed at integrating the needs of wildlife and people, both residents and visitors. The trekking trails are well used, especially during the season (October-November and March-April).

Mammals:

Assam Macaque	Rhesus Macaque	Hanuman Langur
Golden Jackal	Red Fox	Dhole
Asiatic Black Bear	Red Panda	Himalayan Weasel
Yellow-throated Marten	Spotted Linsang	Masked Palm Civet
Leopard Cat	Jungle Cat	Asiatic Golden Cat
Leopard	Snow Leopard	Wild Boar
Forest Musk Deer	Indian Muntjac	Common Goral
Mainland Serow	Himalayan Tahr	Bharal
Black Giant Squirrel	Himalayan Marmot	Royle's Pika

ANNAPURNA CONSERVATION AREA (NEPAL)

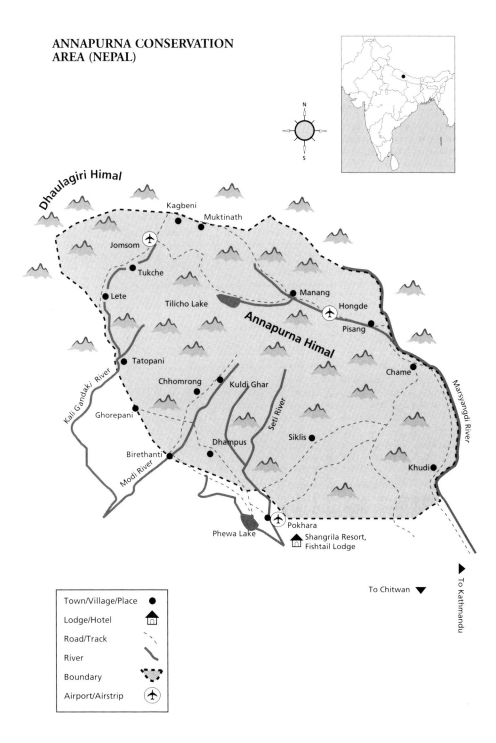

Town/Village/Place ●
Lodge/Hotel
Road/Track
River
Boundary
Airport/Airstrip ✈

2. BANDHAVGARH NATIONAL PARK (INDIA)

Area: 44,884 hectares.
Established: 1968 as a national park. Extended in 1986. 1993 as a tiger reserve.
Description: Bandhavgarh was the former hunting preserve of the Maharaja of Rewa. The famous White Tigers, now major attractions around the world's zoos, were first discovered in Rewa, not far from here. The terrain is broken, with rocky hill ranges, running roughly east-west, interspersed with grassy swamps and forested valleys. The park is dominated by the ancient Bandhavgarh Fort, located on a plateau and reached after a steep climb. The fort is now in ruins, its monuments and tanks beings gradually reclaimed by the forest, thus providing additional shelter for wildlife. Much of the park is covered in Sal forest, replaced by mixed forests in the higher elevations of the hills. There are extensive stands of bamboo and grasslands. Generally the forests are less dense here, with less undergrowth than in North India, thus offering better sightings of wildlife, notably mammals, including the daylight sightings of Tigers in the grassy 'maidans'. 40+ Tigers are estimated for the park. The park also has numerous ancient caves and rock shelters, with shrines and inscriptions. About 240 species of birds are known from the Tala area, including the Brown Fish Owl, Grey-headed Fishing Eagle, Malabar Pied Hornbill and Shahin Falcon.
Season: Mid November to mid June, the best period being January-April.
Access: Fly from Delhi, Agra or Varanasi to Khajuraho and drive (5 hours) to Tala park entrance at Bandhavgarh. Alternatively, take the overnight train from Delhi to Umaria and drive (45 minutes) to the park.
Accommodation and facilities: Most of the tourist accommodation is available at or near Tala. The popular mid-range White Tiger Lodge is run by Madhya Pradesh Tourism. Nearby is the well-established Bandhavgarh Jungle Camp, incorporating safari tents and 4 rooms at the Maharaja's old hunting lodge. Others include Nature Heritage, Bandhavgarh Jungle Lodge and Tiger Trails Resort. Wildlife safaris are in 4-wheel drive motor vehicles and riding elephants are available for tiger sightings at the park office at Tala. To visit Bandhavgarh Fort requires a short drive from Tala and a walk up the hill.

Mammals:

Rhesus Macaque	Hanuman Langur	Golden Jackal
Wolf	Bengal Fox	Dhole
Sloth Bear	Ratel	Small Indian Civet
Common Palm Civet	Small Indian Mongoose	Indian Grey Mongoose
Ruddy Mongoose	Striped Hyaena	Jungle Cat
Leopard	Tiger	Wild Boar
Indian Muntjac	Chital	Sambar
Nilgai	Four-horned Antelope	Gaur
Blackbuck	Indian Gazelle	Indian Pangolin
Northern Palm Squirrel	Indian Porcupine	Indian Hare

BANDHAVGARH NATIONAL PARK (INDIA)

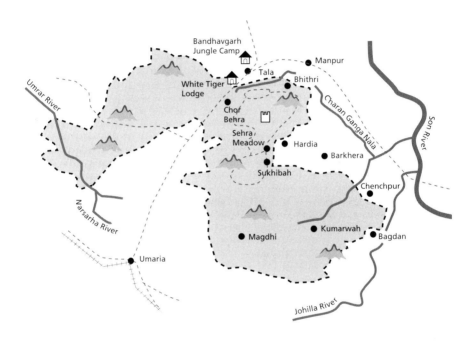

Bandhavgarh Jungle Camp

Manpur

White Tiger Lodge

Tala

Bhithri

Umrar River

Chor Behra

Charan Ganga Nala

Son River

Sehra Meadow

Hardia

Barkhera

Sukhibah

Chenchpur

Narsarha River

Kumarwah

Magdhi

Bagdan

Umaria

Johilla River

Town/Village/Place	●
Lodge/Hotel	
Road/Track	
River	
Boundary	
Fort	
Railway	++++

3. BARDIA NATIONAL PARK (NEPAL)

Area: 96,800 hectares.

Established: 1976 as a wildlife reserve, 1985 as a national park.

Description: Bardia national park is mainly lowland, with the Churia Range of low hills forming its northern boundary. It is drained by the Karnali and the Babai rivers. The vegetation is tropical moist deciduous. In the lowlands, which are subject to flooding during the monsoon, there are riverine forests of Simal, Khair and Sisau that alternate with tall and short grasslands, known locally as 'phantas'. On the well-drained higher ground are forests dominated by the stately Sal, often draped in giant creepers. The forest floor is punctuated with many tall termite mounds. In the mid 1980s Indian Rhinoceros was reintroduced in Bardia from Chitwan and there is now a thriving population of some 40 animals. Recently Bardia has seen an influx of Indian Elephant, possibly from adjoining areas, including a massive male, the Raja Gaj, with a pronounced domed head, presumed to exceed 3.3 metres (11 feet) at the shoulder. Bardia also has both Marsh and Gharial Crocodiles. Mahseer fish are found in the Karnali river.

Season: November-June, the best period being February-April.

Access: Bardia lies some 400 km to the west of Kathmandu, the capital of Nepal. Fly from Kathmandu to Nepalganj and drive to Bardia (2-3 hours to the park headquarters at Thakurdwara).

Accommodation and facilities: There are 2 outstanding places to stay in Bardia: Karnali Jungle Lodge, at the edge of the park, near Thakurdwara, and Karnali Tented Camp (inside the park) on the banks of the Karnali river on the western boundary, south of Chisapani. Both are run by Tiger Tops, pioneers of wildlife tourism in Nepal. Wildlife viewing is by riding elephants, 4-wheel drive motor vehicles, boats (both indigenous wooden and inflatable rubber rafts) and on foot. The park has a good network of roads and trails.

Mammals:

Rhesus Macaque	Hanuman Langur	Golden Jackal
Bengal Fox	Dhole	Sloth Bear
Smooth-coated Otter	Small Indian Civet	Large Indian Civet
Small Indian Mongoose	Indian Grey Mongoose	Striped Hyaena
Leopard Cat	Jungle Cat	Fishing Cat
Leopard	Tiger	Ganges Dolphin
Indian Elephant	Indian Rhinoceros	Wild Boar
Indian Muntjac	Chital	Swamp Deer
Hog Deer	Sambar	Nilgai
Common Goral	Indian Porcupine	Northern Palm Squirrel
Red Giant Flying Squirrel	Hispid Hare	Indian Hare

Small Indian Mongoose

BARDIA NATIONAL PARK (NEPAL)

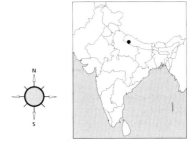

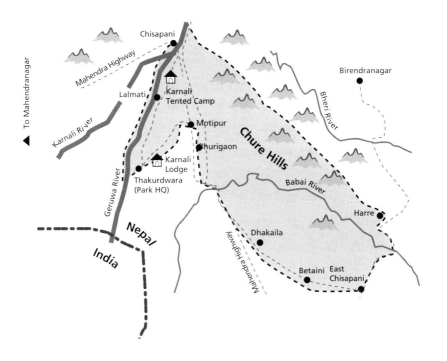

Chisapani

Mahendra Highway

To Mahendranagar

Lalmati

Karnali Tented Camp

Karnali River

Motipur

Jhurigaon

Karnali Lodge

Thakurdwara (Park HQ)

Geruwa River

Birendranagar

Bheri River

Chure Hills

Babai River

Harre

Nepal

India

Dhakaila

Betaini East Chisapani

Mahendra Highway

Town/Village/Place ●

Lodge/Hotel

Road/Track

River

Boundary

International Border

4. CHITWAN NATIONAL PARK (NEPAL)

Area: 93,200 Hectares.

Established: 1962 as a rhinoceros sanctuary, 1973 as a national park.

Description: Chitwan is one of the finest national parks in the Indian subcontinent. Its main attractions are Tiger, Indian Rhinoceros, Gaur and Sloth Bear. The forests are moist deciduous, with the dominant species on the higher ground being the huge Sal. On the ridges of the Churia Hills, Chir Pine trees predominate. On the floodplains of the Rapti, Reu and Narayani rivers there are large areas of tall grasslands, also known as elephant grass. These alternate with patches of riverine forests, with the Simal, Khair and the Sisau trees dominating. Adjoining Chitwan to the east is the Parsa Wildlife Reserve, with 49,900 hectares, and further east, the Bara Hunting Reserve with 25,900 hectares. Contiguous to Chitwan in the south is the Valmiki Tiger Reserve in Bihar, India. Chitwan is a birdwatchers' paradise, with nearly 500 species recorded, and it is possible to see over 100 species in a single day, especially in late February-early March. Other wildlife includes the Marsh Crocodile, Gharial Crocodile and the Indian Python. Rhino sightings in Chitwan are assured.

Season: The park is open year round, but during the monsoon (June-September) the roads inside the park are difficult to negotiate. Best months October-May.

Access: Chitwan lies 100 km to the SW of Kathmandu. Fly from Kathmandu to Meghauli or Bharatpur airports (30 minutes) and drive to the park (1-2 hours). Alternatively, drive from Kathmandu (5-7 hours) or Pokhara (4-6 hours). It is also possible to combine the drives from Kathmandu and Pokhara with a rafting trip on the Trisuli, Seti and Narayani rivers, which can last 1-3 days.

Accommodation and facilities: Chitwan has the widest range of accommodation for foreign tourists anywhere in the subcontinent. Inside the park there are several lodges and camps. The oldest and best known is Tiger Tops which operates a treetop Jungle Lodge and a Tented Camp; it also runs the Tharu Safari Resort, just outside the park. Other lodges inside the park include the Island Jungle Resort, Gaida Wildlife Camp, Machan Wildlife Resort and Temple Tiger. Outside the park there are the Narayani Safari Resort near Kasara and over 30 lodges and camps catering to every budget, mostly located in the Sauraha area. There is a visitor information centre and the government elephant camp at Sauraha. Safaris in the park are by riding elephants (maintained by most good lodges and the government elephant camp at Sauraha), 4-wheel drive motor vehicles, indigenous wooden boats and dugout canoes, and on foot. There are also a number of 'machans' or watch-towers in different parts of the park.

Mammals:

Rhesus Macaque	Hanuman Langur	Golden Jackal
Bengal Fox	Dhole	Sloth Bear
Yellow-throated Marten	Ratel	Smooth-coated Otter
Small Indian Civet	Large Indian Civet	Spotted Linsang
Common Palm Civet	Binturong	Small Indian Mongoose
Indian Grey Mongoose	Crab-eating Mongoose	Striped Hyaena
Leopard Cat	Jungle Cat	Marbled Cat
Fishing Cat	Leopard	Tiger
Ganges Dolphin	Indian Elephant	Indian Rhinoceros
Wild Boar	Indian Muntjac	Chital
Hog Deer	Sambar	Four-horned Antelope
Gaur	Mainland Serow	Indian Pangolin
Northern Palm Squirrel	Red Giant Flying Squirrel	Particoloured Flying Squirrel
Indian Porcupine	Hispid Hare	Indian Hare

CHITWAN NATIONAL PARK (NEPAL)

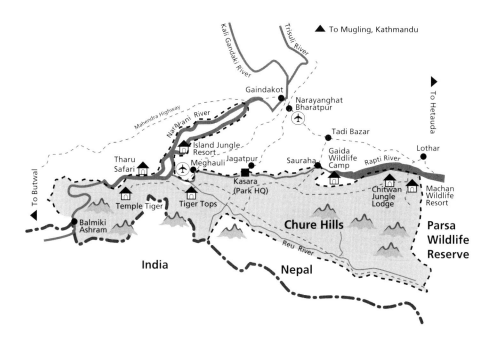

To Mugling, Kathmandu

Kali Gandaki River

Trisuli River

Gaindakot

Narayanghat
Bharatpur

To Hetauda

Mahendra Highway

Narayani River

Tadi Bazar

Island Jungle
Resort

Lothar

Tharu
Safari

Jagatpur

Meghauli

Saurah a

Gaida
Wildlife
Camp

Rapti River

To Butwal

Kasara
(Park HQ)

Chitwan
Jungle
Lodge

Machan
Wildlife
Resort

Temple Tiger

Tiger Tops

Balmiki
Ashram

Chure Hills

**Parsa
Wildlife
Reserve**

India

Reu River

Nepal

Town/Village/Place	●
Lodge/Hotel	
Road/Track	
River	
Boundary	
International
Border	
Airport	✈

5. CORBETT NATIONAL PARK (INDIA)

Area: 52,082 hectares.

Established: 1936 as a national park, India's first (named Hailey National Park; in 1957 renamed Corbett National Park), 1973 as a tiger reserve.

Description: Corbett, where Project Tiger was launched in 1973, is regarded as India's finest national park and its major attractions are the Tiger, Indian Elephant and Leopard. Corbett is drained by the Ramganga river, the dam at Kalagarh forming a huge lake to the west of the park. The park is essentially a large low valley. A range of hills runs through the middle of the park, roughly east to west. The forests are moist deciduous, with Sal as the dominant tree. Chir Pine trees are to be found on the higher ridges of the hills. On the low-lying areas riverine forests, with Shisham and Khair trees, are intermixed with grasslands known locally as 'chaurs'. Along the high banks between Dhangarhi Gate and Dhikala there are several large pools where the Marsh Crocodile and the Gharial Crocodile may be seen. Corbett is also an outstanding place for birdwatching, with over 500 species recorded.

Season: Mid November-Mid June, the best period being February-April.

Access: Corbett lies some 300 km to the NE of Delhi. From Delhi drive to Corbett (6-7 hours). The nearest airport is Pantnagar (2.5 hours) and the nearest railway station is Ramnagar (2 hours from Dhikala).

Accommodation and facilities: The Dhikala Tourist Complex inside the park, run by the Forest Department, has basic accommodation but is a good area for wildlife sightings. Outside the park there are several lodges and camps. The Corbett Lodge has an excellent location being near the Amdanda entry point. Other good accommodation includes Corbett Riverside Resort, Corbett Hideaway and the Quality Inn Corbett Jungle Resort. Safaris by 4-wheel drive motor vehicles. Riding elephants are also available at Dhikala and Bijrani. Day trips to Dhikala from outside the park are not permitted.

Mammals:

Rhesus Macaque	Hanuman Langur	Golden Jackal
Red Fox	Dhole	Asiatic Black Bear
Sloth Bear	Yellow-throated Marten	Eurasian Otter
Small Indian Civet	Spotted Linsang	Common Palm Civet
Masked Palm Civet	Indian Grey Mongoose	Leopard Cat
Jungle Cat	Tiger	Indian Elephant
Wild Boar	Indian Muntjac	Chital
Hog Deer	Sambar	Nilgai
Common Goral	Indian Pangolin	Northern Palm Squirrel
Red Giant Flying Squirrel	Indian Porcupine	Indian Hare

Common Palm Civet

86

CORBETT NATIONAL PARK (INDIA)

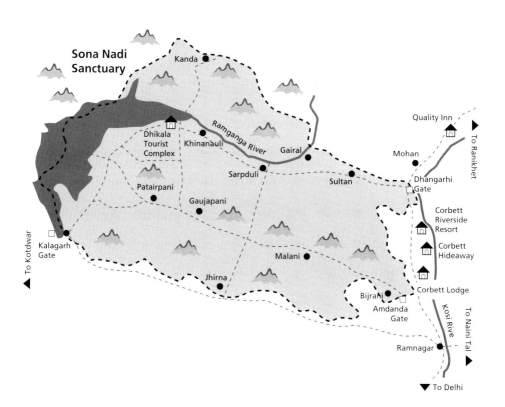

Sona Nadi Sanctuary

Kanda

Ramganga River

Dhikala Tourist Complex

Khinanauli

Gairal

Quality Inn

To Ranikhet

Mohan

Sarpduli

Sultan

Dhangarhi Gate

Patairpani

Gaujapani

Corbett Riverside Resort

Corbett Hideaway

To Kotdwar

Kalagarh Gate

Malani

Corbett Lodge

Jhirna

Bijrani

Amdanda Gate

Kosi River

To Naini Tal

Ramnagar

To Delhi

Town/Village/Place	●
Lodge/Hotel	🏠
Road/Track	
River	
Boundary	

6. DACHIGAM NATIONAL PARK (INDIA)

Area: 14,100 hectares.

Established: 1951 as a sanctuary, 1981 as a national park.

Description: Dachigam is best known for its Red Deer or the Kashmir Stag, known locally as the Hangul (park population estimated at 290 in 1995). The park is mountainous (part of the Zanskar Range) and lies between two high mountain ridges with numerous gulleys. In Lower Dachigam there are extensive riverine forests with Kashmir Elm, Poplar and Willow. During August and September, there are excellent chances of seeing the Asiatic Black Bear feeding here. Higher, there are forests of Blue Pine, Silver Fir, Birch and Rhododendron, and, between 3,200-3,700 metres elevation, evergreen shrubs. High in Upper Dachigam lies the huge Marsar Lake which feeds the Daghwan river that flows through the park into the Harwan reservoir, the main source of drinking water in Srinagar. The area was given protection by the Maharaja of Jammu and Kashmir in 1910, largely to preserve its watershed areas. In the ensuing 24 years, 10 villages were relocated outside the sanctuary, hence its name Dachi = ten, gam = villages. More than 150 species of birds are found in the park, including the Himalayan Griffon and Lammergeier. The streams have Rainbow Trout.

Season: Open year round, the best period being May-September.

Access: Dachigam has easy access, being only 32 km by road from Srinagar, the capital of Jammu and Kashmir, to the park entrance at Harwan.

Accommodation and facilities: For day visitors, it is best to stay in one of many houseboats in the Dal or Nagin lakes or in a hotel in Srinagar. There is a VIP Lodge at Draphama run by the government. However, Dachigam is best explored trekking, following known trails and staying overnight in tents. There are some motorable roads also.

Mammals:

Hanuman Langur	Golden Jackal	Red Fox
Asiatic Black Bear	Brown Bear	Himalayan Weasel
Yellow-throated Marten	Eurasian Otter	Leopard Cat
Jungle Cat	Leopard	Snow Leopard
Wild Boar	Forest Musk Deer	Red Deer
Mainland Serow	Long-tailed Marmot	

Yellow-throated Marten

88

DACHIGAM NATIONAL PARK (INDIA)

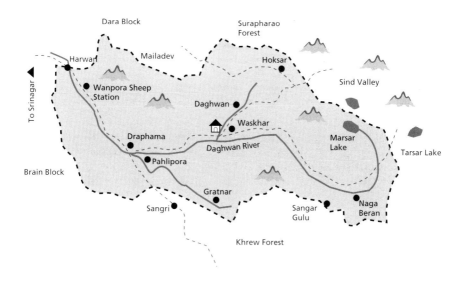

Dara Block

Surapharao Forest

Harwan

Mailadev

Hoksar

Sind Valley

To Srinagar

Wanpora Sheep Station

Daghwan

Waskhar

Draphama

Daghwan River

Marsar Lake

Tarsar Lake

Brain Block

Pahlipora

Gratnar

Sangri

Sangar Gulu

Naga Beran

Khrew Forest

Town/Village/Place	●
Lodge/Hotel	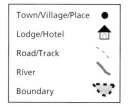
Road/Track	
River	
Boundary	

7. DUDHWA NATIONAL PARK (INDIA)

Area: 49,029 hectares.
Established: 1958 as a wildlife sanctuary, 1977 as a national park, 1988 as a tiger reserve.
General: Dudhwa lies on the India-Nepal border in the foothills of the Himalaya and the plains of the 'terai'. The main attractions of the park are its Swamp Deer (population over 1,600) and Tiger (population 98 in 1995). The park is famous for the untiring efforts of 'Billy' Arjan Singh, one of India's leading conservationists, who was instrumental in the creation of Dudhwa as a sanctuary for the protection of the Swamp Deer. Later he successfully hand-reared and re-introduced zoo-born Tigers and Leopards into the wilds of Dudhwa. The forests here are reminiscent of the forests of Bardia on the Nepal side, with huge Sal trees, tall termite mounds, patches of riverine forests and large open grasslands. Its lakes offer excellent opportunities for observing Swamp Deer and birds from 'machans'. In the mid 1980s, Indian Rhinoceros was reintroduced into Dudhwa from Assam and Nepal. The park has a rich birdlife, with over 350 species, including the Swamp Partridge, Slaty-backed Woodpecker and Bengal Florican.
Season: Mid November-mid June, the best period being February-April.
Access: Drive from Delhi (8-9 hours) or take the train to Shahjehanpur and drive to Dudhwa (3 hours). Alternatively fly to Lucknow and drive to Dudhwa (245 km, 6 hours).
Accommodation and facilities: At the southern edge of the park lies the well-known Tiger Haven, the residence of 'Billy' Arjan Singh and open to tourists. It is a rustic farm house with good accommodation and is well placed for productive safaris inside the park. Safaris are by 4-wheel drive motor vehicles and by elephants. There is also a Forest Rest House inside the park.

Mammals:

Rhesus Macaque	Hanuman Langur	Golden Jackal
Wolf	Bengal Fox	Sloth Bear
Ratel	Eurasian Otter	Smooth-coated Otter
Small Indian Civet	Spotted Linsang	Small Indian Mongoose
Indian Grey Mongoose	Striped Hyaena	Leopard Cat
Jungle Cat	Fishing Cat	Leopard
Tiger	Indian Elephant	Indian Rhinoceros
Wild Boar	Indian Muntjac	Chital
Swamp Deer	Hog Deer	Sambar
Nilgai	Four-horned Antelope	Blackbuck
Indian Pangolin	Northern Palm Squirrel	Red Giant Flying Squirrel
Indian Porcupine	Hispid Hare	Indian Hare

Small Indian Civet

DUDHWA NATIONAL PARK (INDIA)

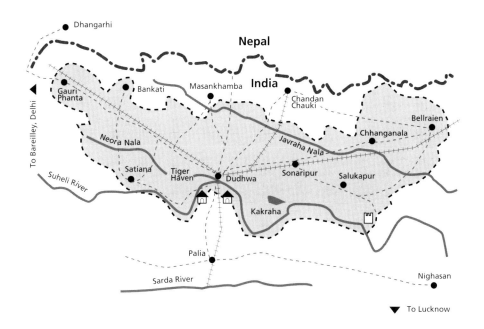

Dhangarhi

Nepal

Gauri Phanta

Bankati

Masankhamba

India

Chandan Chauki

Bellraien

To Bareilley, Delhi

Neora Nala

Chhanganala

Suheli River

Satiana

Tiger Haven

Dudhwa

Javraha Nala

Sonaripur

Salukapur

Kakraha

Palia

Sarda River

Nighasan

To Lucknow

Town/Village/Place	●
Lodge/Hotel	
Road/Track	
River	
Boundary	
Fort	
International Border	

8. GIR NATIONAL PARK (INDIA)

Area: Lion sanctuary 141,213 hectares, of which national park 35,948 hectares.
Established: 1966 as a sanctuary, 1975 as a national park.
Description: Gir is the only home in India of the Lion of which there are nearly 300 in the park. The sanctuary lies in the Gujarat peninsula in SW India. The terrain is rugged with low hills and the vegetation is mixed deciduous, with stands of Teak, Acacia, Jamun, Tendu and Dhak trees, interspersed with large patches of grasslands. On the hills the trees are sparse and stunted. Within the sanctuary, there are numerous human settlements of cattle herders called Maldharis with an estimated 20,000 head of livestock (which, incidentally, forms a significant part of the Lion's diet). There are also places of Hindu worship and pilgrimage and sulphur springs at Tulsi Shyam and Kankai Mata. At the edge of the park there are good populations of Indian Gazelle, protected by the religious sentiment of the local people. The Kamleshwar Lake has some Marsh Crocodile. Birds in the park include the Paradise Flycatcher, Bonelli's Eagle and Painted Sandgrouse.
Season: Mid October-mid June, best period being December-April.
Access: Drive to Gir from Keshod (90 km) or Rajkot (166 km) airports. There is also a railway station at Sasan Gir.
Accommodation and facilities: The Gir Lodge has recently been refurbished and upgraded. Nearby is the family-run Maneland Lodge, suitable for small groups. Safaris are by 4-wheel drive motor vehicles.

Mammals:

Hanuman Langur	Golden Jackal	Bengal Fox
Small Indian Civet	Small Indian Mongoose	Indian Grey Mongoose
Striped Hyaena	Jungle Cat	Rusty-spotted Cat
Wild Cat	Lion	Leopard
Wild Boar	Chital	Sambar
Nilgai	Four-horned Antelope	Indian Gazelle
Indian Pangolin	Northern Palm Squirrel	Indian Porcupine
Indian Hare		

Striped Hyaena

GIR NATIONAL PARK (INDIA)

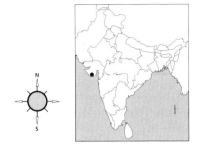

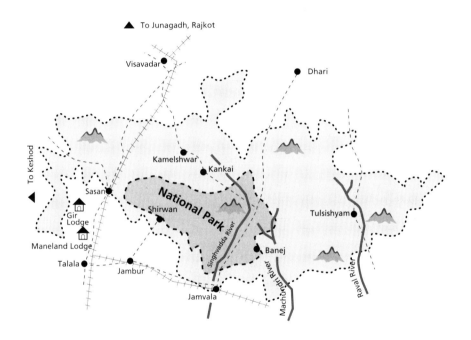

▲ To Junagadh, Rajkot

Visavadar

Dhari

To Keshod

Kamelshwar
Kankai

Sasan

National Park

Shirwan

Gir
Lodge

Tulsishyam

Maneland Lodge

Talala
Jambur

Banej

Jamvala

Singhvadda River

Machundri River

Raval River

Town/Village/Place	●
Lodge/Hotel	🏠
Road/Track	
River	
Boundary	
Railway	++++

9. HEMIS NATIONAL PARK (INDIA)

Area: 410,000 hectares (core 125,000 hectares). Further extensions proposed.
Established: 1981 as a national park.
Description: Hemis National Park is one of the largest protected areas in the Indian Himalaya. The park derives its name from the nearby Hemis Gompa, Ladakh's largest and most important Buddhist monastery. Hemis is situated to the west and southwest of Leh, the capital of Ladakh, and extends from the southern banks of the Indus river to the Tsarap river on the Zanskar Range. The terrain is mountainous throughout, with elevations varying from 3,300 to 6,400 metres. The park is representative of the transhimalayan high-altitude deserts of Central Ladakh. It hardly rains here, with annual precipitation being 2 cm, so the skies are deep blue and generally clear. The landscape is incredibly beautiful, with various shades of pastel, although the park is largely barren, with sparse vegetation. There are patches of grasslands and shrubs, and some open forests and woodlands along the rivers. Trees include species of Juniper, Birch and Poplar. The local people also grow Willow, Apple and Apricot. Alpine species grow above the tree line at about 4,500 metres up to the snow line at 5,000 metres. The main attractions of the park are Bharal and Snow Leopard. Sighting mammals is not easy, however, because of the difficult mountainous terrain, the shy nature of its mammals and camouflage afforded by the landscape.
Season: May-October, best period being July-September.
Access: Fly from Delhi or Srinagar to Leh and proceed to the park by road (40 km) and on foot. Ponies and domestic yaks are available as beasts of burden. When flying into Leh it is important to spend 2-4 days in Leh acclimatising to the high altitude before venturing into Hemis national park.
Accommodation and facilities: There are no permanent lodges and camps inside the park. It is best to organise a trek into Hemis generally following the old trading/trekking trails and staying overnight in tents. There are a number of tourist hotels and lodges in Leh. The Ladakh Sarai, consisting of 'yurts' or Central Asian yak-hair tents, is at the edge of Stok village. Riding ponies are available, but it is best to explore the park on foot.

Mammals:

Wolf	Red Fox	Dhole
Brown Bear	Himalayan Weasel	Beech Marten
Eurasian Otter	Eurasian Lynx	Pallas's Cat
Snow Leopard	Bharal	Long-tailed Marmot
Himalayan Marmot	Royle's Pika	

Dhole

HEMIS NATIONAL PARK (INDIA)

▲ To Nubra Valley

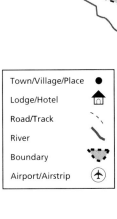

Leh

Indus River

Ladakh Sarai   Shey

Stok   Matho   Thiksey

Hemis

Zanskar River

Chang Chu

Shang River

Gya

Zangla

Niri Chu

Padum

Shadi   Karnak

Tantak

Tsarap Chu

Zara River

Shun

Town/Village/Place	●
Lodge/Hotel	
Road/Track	
River	
Boundary	
Airport/Airstrip	✈

▼ To Manali

10. KANHA NATIONAL PARK (INDIA)

Area: 94,000 hectares of national park, surrounded by 100,500 hectares of additional buffer area.

Established: 1933 as a sanctuary, 1955 as a national park, 1973 as a tiger reserve.

General: Kanha and the nearby forests were the setting for The Jungle Book by Rudyard Kipling. Kanha is the outstanding national park of Central India, noted for its last remaining population of the hard-ground race of the Swamp Deer (approximately 380). It also has healthy numbers of the Tiger, which may be seen during the day, and is one of the best places left to see them. Kanha has two main valleys, Halon in the east and Banjar in the west, and the grassy 'maidans' (often old village sites), dotted with clumps of forest, harbour large numbers of herbivores. The hills often support sizeable plateaus (locally called 'dadars') and are characterised by extensive grasslands and scant trees. These 'dadars' are much favoured by Gaur and Four-horned Antelope. The forests are deciduous, the main tree being the Sal, and there are large stands of bamboo. Higher up the slopes the forests tend to become dense and mixed with Haldu and Bija trees. Birds in the park include the Painted Partridge, Shaheen Falcon and Golden Oriole.

Season: November-June, the best period being February-April.

Access: Drive from Jabalpur (6 hours), which is also the nearest airport and railway station, or from Nagpur (7 hours).

Accommodation and facilities: At the park entrance at Kisli are the Baghira Log Huts run by Madhya Pradesh Tourism. There are a number of private lodges and camps outside the park near Kisli, including Kipling Camp, run by old Indophiles Bob and Ann Wright, and Wild Chalet Lodge. Near the Mukki entrance are Kanha Safari Lodge and Kanha Jungle Lodge. Safaris are by 4-wheel drive motor vehicles. Elephant rides are available from Kisli and Mukki park offices.

Mammals:

Rhesus Macaque	Hanuman Langur	Golden Jackal
Wolf	Bengal Fox	Dhole
Sloth Bear	Smooth-coated Otter	Ratel
Small Indian Civet	Indian Grey Mongoose	Ruddy Mongoose
Striped Hyaena	Jungle Cat	Leopard
Tiger	Indian Spotted Chevrotain	Wild Boar
Indian Muntjac	Chital	Swamp Deer
Sambar	Nilgai	Four-horned Antelope
Gaur	Blackbuck	Indian Pangolin
Indian Palm Squirrel	Indian Porcupine	Indian Hare

Indian Porcupine

96

KANHA NATIONAL PARK (INDIA)

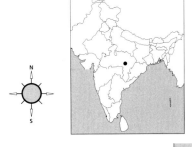

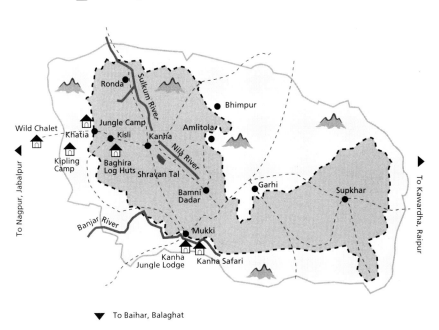

▲ To Motinala, Mandla

Ronda

Sulkum River

Bhimpur

Wild Chalet

Jungle Camp

Khatia

Amlitola

Kisli

Kanha

Nila River

To Nagpur, Jabalpur

Kipling Camp

Baghira Log Huts

Shravan Tal

Bamni Dadar

Garhi

Supkhar

To Kawardha, Raipur

Banjar River

Mukki

Kanha Jungle Lodge

Kanha Safari

▼ To Baihar, Balaghat

Town/Village/Place	●
Lodge/Hotel	
Road/Track	
River	
Boundary	

97

11. KAZIRANGA NATIONAL PARK (INDIA)

Area: 42,996 hectares.

Established: 1926 as a reserve forest, 1940 as a wildlife sanctuary, 1974 as a national park.

Description: Kaziranga National Park lies to the south of the mighty Brahmaputra river and being on the floodplains is inundated heavily by the monsoon rains. The predominant vegetation is a mixture of tall grasslands and riverine forests. There are many marshes, interconnecting streams and ox-bow lakes, known locally as 'bheels' or 'bils'. To the south of the park lie the Mikir Hills which rise to over 1,000 metres elevation. Kaziranga is famous for its Indian Rhinoceros population which is estimated at 1,100+ and is by far the best place to see them in India. (This species is unique to the subcontinent, with the second largest population of 400+ found in Chitwan, Nepal). Other large mammals include the Water Buffalo, Swamp Deer and Gangetic Dolphin. The park may be explored by riding elephant or 4-wheel drive motor vehicles. There are several watch towers. The nearby Panbari Reserve Forest is the best place to see the Hoolock Gibbon. Kaziranga has a rich birdlife. There is a colony of Spot-billed Pelicans and the rare Bengal Floricans inhabit the grasslands. This area is also known for the famous Assam tea and during the winter and spring it is worthwhile visiting the nearby tea plantations to see tea leaves being picked and processed.

Season: November-May, the best period being January-April.

Access: Drive to the park from Gauhati (219 km, 6 hours) or Jorhat (96 km, 2 hours) airports, accessible by flights from Delhi and Calcutta respectively. The nearest railway station is Jakhalabandha (43 km).

Accommodation and facilities: The Aranya Forest Lodge and two tourist lodges run by the Assam government are 3 km from the park entrance at Mihimukh. The Wild Grass Lodge is located a little further. Riding elephants are available at the Mihimukh entrance.

Mammals:

Assam Macaque	Hoolock Gibbon	Capped Langur
Golden Jackal	Bengal Fox	Dhole
Asiatic Black Bear	Sloth Bear	Yellow-throated Marten
Smooth-coated Otter	Small Indian Civet	Large Indian Civet
Common Palm Civet	Small Indian Mongoose	Indian Grey Mongoose
Leopard Cat	Jungle Cat	Fishing Cat
Leopard	Tiger	Ganges Dolphin
Indian Elephant	Indian Rhinoceros	Wild Boar
Indian Muntjac	Swamp Deer	Hog Deer
Sambar	Water Buffalo	Gaur
Indian Pangolin	Black Giant Squirrel	Indian Porcupine
Orange-bellied	Indian Hare	Himalayan Squirrel

Large Indian Civet

KAZIRANGA NATIONAL PARK (INDIA)

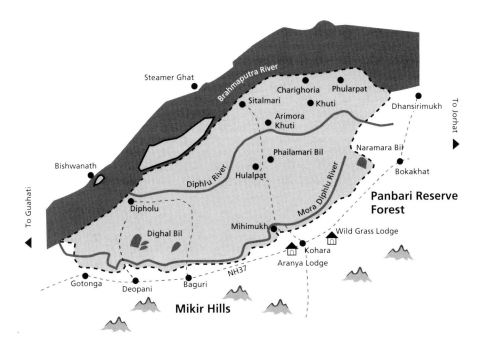

Steamer Ghat

Brahmaputra River

Charighoria Phularpat
Sitalmari
Khuti
Dhansirimukh
Arimora
Khuti

Phailamari Bil
Naramara Bil

Bishwanath
Diphlu River
Hulalpat
Bokakhat

To Guahati

Dipholu
Mora Diphlu River

Panbari Reserve
Forest

Dighal Bil
Mihimukh
Wild Grass Lodge

Kohara
Aranya Lodge

Gotonga
Deopani
Baguri
NH37

Mikir Hills

To Jorhat

Town/Village/Place	●
Lodge/Hotel	🏠
Road/Track	
River	
Boundary	

99

12. KEOLADEO GHANA OR BHARATPUR NATIONAL PARK (INDIA)

Area: 2,873 hectares.

Established: 1956 as a bird sanctuary, 1981 as a national park.

Description: The marshes of Keoladeo, more popularly known as Bharatpur, was the private hunting reserve of the Maharajas of Bharatpur. It was developed in the late 19th century by creating small dams and bunds in an area of natural depression to collect rainwater and by feeding it with an irrigation canal. Over the years, the lakes attracted great numbers of waterfowl and the Maharajas held grand shoots with family, friends and visiting dignitaries. Two-thirds of the park lies under water, the extent and volume depending on the intensity of the rains. The remaining one-third of the park is covered in dry deciduous forests (with Acacia, Ber, Kadam and Khajur trees) and extensive grasslands. On the raised ground outlining the wetlands grow a profusion of Acacia trees, where the resident water birds nest, often in large mixed colonies, a spectacular sight during the monsoon. Keoladeo is famous as one of Asia's finest birding areas, with over 380 resident and migrant species, including the Common, Demoiselle and the rare Siberian Cranes. It is also an excellent place to watch mammals like Golden Jackal, Striped Hyaena, Fishing Cat, Jungle Cat, Nilgai, Sambar, Blackbuck and Wild Boar. The park derives its name from the temple of Keoladeo (Shiva) and 'ghana' which locally means dense, implying the nature of the vegetation. During the cool winter months it is also possible to see large Indian Pythons sunning themselves.

Season: The park is open throughout the year. Best months are August-November for resident breeding birds and November-March for migrant birds.

Access: Bharatpur is well connected by road from Agra (56 km, 1 hour), Delhi (176 km, 5 hours) and Jaipur (176 km, 6 hours), all of which have airports. The Bharatpur railway station is 6 km from the park.

Accommodation and facilities: The popular Bharatpur Forest Lodge run by India Tourism is inside the park. Outside the park, there are the Laxmi Vilas Palace, Saras Lodge, Hotel Sunbird, and a number of other lodges. The Golbagh Palace is scheduled to open in 1997. It is also possible to make day trips to Keoladeo from Agra, where there are several good hotels; or from Fatehpur Sikri, which has the Gulistan Hotel. The park may be explored by cycle-rickshaw, boat and on foot. Pedal bicycles may also be hired from suppliers through the lodges and hotels.

Mammals:

Rhesus Macaque	Golden Jackal	Bengal Fox
Smooth-coated Otter	Small Indian Civet	Common Palm Civet
Small Indian Mongoose	Indian Grey Mongoose	Striped Hyaena
Jungle Cat	Fishing Cat	Wild Boar
Chital	Sambar	Nilgai
Blackbuck	Northern Palm Squirrel	Indian Porcupine
Indian Hare		

Northern Palm Squirrel

KEOLADEO GHANA OR BHARATPUR
NATIONAL PARK (INDIA)

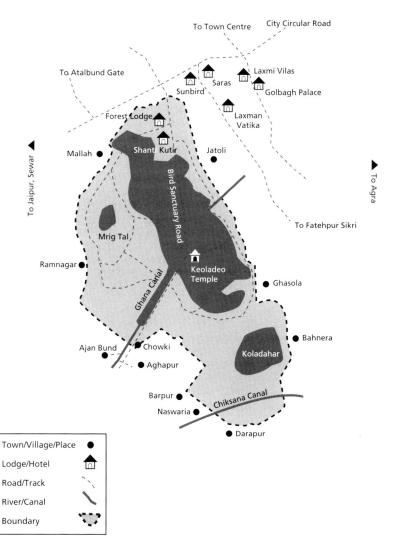

13. MANAS NATIONAL PARK (BHUTAN) and MANAS NATIONAL PARK (INDIA)

Area: Bhutan 65,800 hectares. India 39,100 hectares.
Established: In Bhutan, 1966 as a wildlife sanctuary, 1988 as a national park. In India, 1928 as a reserve forest, 1973 as a tiger reserve.
General: The Manas National Parks in Bhutan and India are the only known homes for the Golden Leaf Monkey, discovered a few decades ago. The Bhutan Manas has some 1,000 Golden Leaf Monkeys, the Indian side having only a small fraction of that number. The two Manas parks are contiguous and together form a relatively secure habitat for its wildlife. Manas has a large variety of mammals, including the rare and endangered Hispid Hare and Pygmy Hog. Larger mammals include Indian Elephant, Gaur, Water Buffalo and Indian Rhinoceros. In Bhutan, much of the park straddles the outer Himalayan foothills, covered in dense tropical (up to 1,000 metres), subtropical (1,000-2,000 metres) and montane (2,000-3,000 metres) forests. Along the Manas river and its tributaries fine stands of riverine forests are to be found, as well as tall grasslands on the floodplains. To the south of the border, the Indian Manas has tropical forests on high ground and riverine forests and tall grasslands on the lower plains. Manas is also rich in birds. The large numbers of Hornbills flying over the Manas river in the early mornings and the evenings are a spectacular sight.
Season: November-May, the best period being January-April.
Access: The Bhutan Manas is not easily accessible and involves long drives. For the Indian Manas the nearest airport is Gauhati (176 km, 6 hours) and the nearest railway station Barpeta Road (40 km from the Bansbari entrance).
Accommodation and facilities: In the Bhutan Manas there is a small guest house at the park headquarters, run by Bhutan Tourism. In the Indian Manas there is a Forest and

Clouded Leopard

MANAS NATIONAL PARK (BHUTAN)

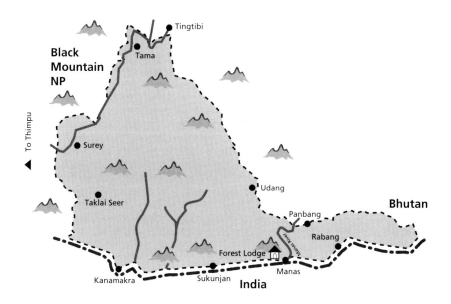

Tingtibi

Black Mountain NP

Tama

To Thimpu

Surey

Taklai Seer

Udang

Panbang

Bhutan

Rabang

Forest Lodge

Manas

Kanamakra

Sukunjan

India

Town/Village/Place	●
Lodge/Hotel	
Road/Track	
River	
Boundary	
International Border	

Tourist Rest House inside the park at Mothanguri, from where riding elephants are available. The Golden Langur Resort is situated near the park entrance at Bansbari. It is possible to venture into the Bhutan side from the Indian Manas (although this may not be strictly permissible).

Mammals:

Slow Loris	Assam Macaque	Rhesus Macaque
Golden Leaf Monkey	Capped Leaf Monkey	Golden Jackal
Wolf (Bhutan)	Bengal Fox	Dhole
Asiatic Black Bear (Bhutan)	Sloth Bear	Yellow-bellied Weasel
Yellow-throated Marten	Eurasian Otter	Small Indian Civet
Large Indian Civet	Common Palm Civet	Masked Palm Civet
Binturong	Small Indian Mongoose	Leopard Cat
Jungle Cat	Marbled Cat	Fishing Cat
Asiatic Golden Cat (Bhutan)	Leopard	Tiger
Clouded Leopard	Ganges Dolphin	Indian Elephant
Indian Rhinoceros	Pygmy Hog	Wild Boar
Indian Muntjac	Chital	Swamp Deer
Hog Deer	Sambar	Water Buffalo
Gaur	Mainland Serow (Bhutan)	Indian Pangolin
Black Giant Squirrel	Hispid Hare	Indian Hare

Leopard Cat

MANAS NATIONAL PARK (INDIA)

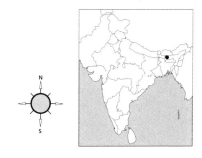

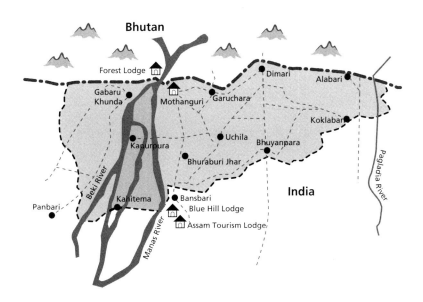

Bhutan

Forest Lodge

Gabaru
Khunda

Mothanguri

Garuchara

Dimari

Alabari

Koklabari

Kapurpura

Uchila

Bhuyanpara

Bhuraburi Jhar

Beki River

Kahitema

Panbari

Bansbari

Blue Hill Lodge

Assam Tourism Lodge

Manas River

India

Pagladia River

Town/Village/Place

Lodge/Hotel

Road/Track

River

Boundary

International
Border

14. NAGARHOLE, BANDIPUR AND MUDUMALAI NATIONAL PARKS (INDIA)

Area: Nagarhole 64,330 hectares. Bandipur 87,420 hectares. Mudumalai 32,155 hectares.
Established: Nagarhole, 1955 as a sanctuary, 1975 as a national park. Bandipur, 1931 as a sanctuary, 1941 as a national park, 1973 as a tiger reserve. Mudumalai, 1940 as a sanctuary.
Description: The national parks of Nagarhole, Bandipur and Mudumalai are contiguous and share very similar characteristics. A fourth national park, Wynad, also adjoins them. Together they form the largest protected area for the Indian Elephant, Gaur, Tiger and Leopard in South India. Other large mammals include Liontail Macaque, Wild Boar and Sambar. The parks occupy a NW-SE alignment, with Nagarhole at the top, Bandipur in the middle, and Mudumalai at the bottom. The forests are tropical mixed deciduous. In the northern and western parts of Nagarhole, which receive more rainfall, the forests are denser and taller, with hardwood trees like Rosewood, Teak and Mathi. Sandalwood trees also grow here. Elsewhere in Nagarhole, and in Bandipur and Mudumalai, which lie in the rain shadow of the Western Ghats, the forests are more open with more grasslands, and the trees are stunted (hence mammal sightings are less difficult). The drier SE corner of Bandipur has scrub forests. During the dry months of March-May, Indian Elephants stay close to rivers and lakes. At this time of year, Indian Elephant sightings are unsurpassed in Nagarhole, especially if you are staying at the Kabini River Lodge in Karapur. Nearby, at Mastigudi large gatherings of 100 or so Indian Elephants on the banks of the Kabini Lake are known, a sight unrivalled anywhere. Bandipur is probably the best place in the subcontinent for seeing Dhole, and the Indian Giant Squirrel can be seen at Mudumalai, lying curled in tree holes or crooks of branches during the day.
Season: Open year round, the best period being October-May, especially April-May.
Access: Fly to Bangalore and drive to Nagarhole (6 hours) or Bandipur (6-7 hours). The nearest station railway station is Mysore. For Mudumalai the nearest airport is Coimbatore (160 km) and the nearest railway station Ooty or Udhagamandalam (64 km).
Accommodation and facilities: There are a number of forest lodges and rest houses in Nagarhole-Bandipur-Mudumalai. Superior lodges include the Kabini River Lodge run by the Karnataka government at Karapur, at the edge of Nagarhole. The Gateway Tusker Lodge, at Murukal, inside the park, is scheduled to open in 1997. At the edge of Bandipur, which has an excellent network of motorable roads and tracks, there are Bush Betta and Tusker Trails Cottages outside the park and a Forest Rest House at the park entrance. Near Mudumalai, there are Bamboo Banks and Jungle Hut. Riding elephants are available in Bandipur and Mudumalai. Most of the safaris are, however, done by 4-wheel drive vehicles. Buffalo hide coracle boats are available at the Kabini river reservoir at Nagarhole.

Mammals:

Bonnet Macaque	Liontail Macaque	Hanuman Langur
Nilgiri Langur (adjoining areas)	Golden Jackal	Bengal Fox
Dhole	Sloth Bear	Eurasian Otter
Smooth-coated Otter	Oriental Small-clawed Otter	Small Indian Civet
Common Palm Civet	Indian Grey Mongoose	Ruddy Mongoose
Stripe-necked Mongoose	Striped Hyaena	Leopard Cat
Jungle Cat	Rusty-spotted Cat	Leopard
Tiger	Ratel	Indian Elephant
Wild Boar	Indian Spotted Chevrotain	Indian Muntjac
Chital	Sambar	Four-horned Antelope
Gaur	Nilgiri Tahr (adjoining areas)	Indian Pangolin
Indian Palm Squirrel	Indian Giant Squirrel	Red Giant Flying Squirrel
Grizzled Indian Squirrel	Indian Porcupine	Indian Hare

NAGARHOLE, BANDIPUR AND
MUDUMALAI NATIONAL PARKS (INDIA)

Mattigodu

Hunsur

Mysore

Titimati

Tusker Lodge

Mettikoppa

Murkal

Lakshmanatirtha River

Kabini River

Nagarhole

Nagarhole

Kabini Lodge

Nagarhole River

Karapura

Nugu Reservoir

Karnataka

Kerala

Mastigudi

Kandi Betta

Gundlupet

Wynad
Wildlife
Reserve

Bandipur

Mulehole

Forest Rest House

Bush Betta

Sultan's
Battery

Bandipur

Mudumalai

Máyar River

Mudumalai

Masinigudi

Nellakota

Bamboo Banks

Gudalur

Jungle Hut

Tamil Nadu

▼ To Ooty

Town/Village/Place	●
Lodge/Hotel	
Road/Track	
River	
Boundary	

107

15. NAMDAPHA NATIONAL PARK (INDIA)

Area: 180,782 hectares.
Established: 1972 as a national park, 1983 as a tiger reserve.
Description: Namdapha National Park has perhaps the richest diversity of flora and fauna in the Indian subcontinent. This is because of its biogeographical location within the Indo-Chinese subregion and its great altitudinal variation, from 4,500 metres at Daphabum, the highest point, to 200 metres in the lowest valleys. The park is largely mountainous and is drained by the Noa-Dehing, Deban and Namdapha rivers. In the lower levels grow a tangled profusion of tropical rainforests, with huge Hollock, Hollong and Mekai trees intermixed with giant creepers, tall cane and dense bamboo stands. Higher up are the deciduous forests, with temperate and alpine forests higher still, where Oak, Magnolia, Pine, Betula and Rhododendrons grow in profusion. Namdapha is a botanical haven, with over 150 tree species and many flowers and orchids, including the Blue Vanda, one of the rarest orchids. It will be many years before Namdapha's flora is fully surveyed. Namdapha's birdlife includes the Satyr Tragopan, Kalij and Monal Pheasants, Giant Hornbill, Forest Eagle Owl and the rare White-winged Wood Duck. Principal reptiles include the Indian Python, Reticulated Python and King Cobra. For mammal watchers, the park boasts no fewer than four large cats - Tiger, Leopard, Clouded Leopard and Snow Leopard. It also has a good population of the Hoolock Gibbon.
Season: November-May, the best period being December-March.
Access: Drive to the park from Dibrugarh (140 km, 5 hours) or Gauhati (full day) airports, with flights from Calcutta and Delhi respectively. The nearest railway station is at Ledo, near Margherita (56 km).
Accommodation and facilities: There are a few basic rest houses in Namdapha, at Haldibari. Until the infrastructure is established, this park is suited only to the most die-hard mammal watchers. Movement within the park is restricted, as there are very few trails. The vegetation is dense thus limiting movement and visibility. Safaris are by 4-wheel drive vehicles, riding elephants and on foot.
Note: An inner-line permit is required to visit Arunachal Pradesh, which can be obtained from the Home Ministry in New Delhi 8-12 weeks in advance. Apply as early as possible.

Mammals:

Slow Loris	Assam Macaque	Hoolock Gibbon
Capped Leaf Monkey	Golden Jackal	Wolf
Red Fox	Dhole	Asiatic Black Bear
Red Panda	Yellow-throated Marten	Eurasian Otter
Oriental Small-clawed Otter	Small Indian Civet	Large Indian Civet
Spotted Linsang	Common Palm Civet	Masked Palm Civet
Binturong	Small Indian Mongoose	Crab-eating Mongoose
Leopard Cat	Marbled Cat	Asiatic Golden Cat
Fishing Cat	Leopard	Tiger
Snow Leopard	Clouded Leopard	Indian Elephant
Wild Boar	Forest Musk Deer	Indian Muntjac
Hog Deer	Sambar	Gaur
Common Goral	Mainland Serow	Takin
Spotted Giant Flying Squirrel	Black Giant Squirrel	Bharal
Particoloured Flying Squirrel	Hodgson's Short-tailed Porcupine	

NAMDAPHA NATIONAL PARK (INDIA)

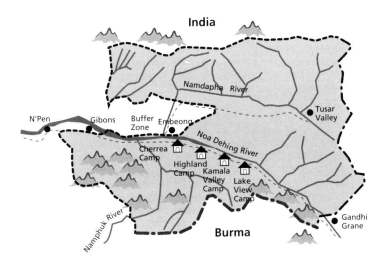

India

Namdapha River

N'Pen   Gibons   Buffer   Emibeong   Tusar Valley
                 Zone
                          Noa Dehing River
                 Cherrea
                 Camp
                     Highland   Kamala
                     Camp   Valley   Lake
                                Camp   View
                                         Camp
                                                 Gandhi
                                                 Grane
Namphuk River

Burma

Town/Village/Place	●
Lodge/Hotel	🏠
Road/Track	
River	
Boundary	
International	
Border	

16. PERIYAR NATIONAL PARK (INDIA)

Area: 77,700 hectares.

Established: 1950 as a sanctuary, 1978 as a tiger reserve.

Description: Periyar National Park is situated in the hills of the Western Ghats in the state of Kerala in SW India. The centrepiece of the park is the 5,500-hectare Periyar Lake formed by the construction of a dam on the Periyar river in 1895. The dam submerged low-lying forest whose dead treetrunks still jut out of the waters. Along the fringes of the lake are marshy areas with tall grasslands. This is one of the richest habitats for large mammals, as it provides both excellent cover and nourishment in the form of succulent shoots and grasses. Here it is possible to see large herds of Indian Elephant with relative ease as well as Nilgiri Langur near Aranya Niwas and the Liontail Macaque in higher areas. The forests are tropical, a mixture of deciduous, semi-evergreen, and evergreen 'sholas', the last occurring in the moist valleys and characterised by tall trees and a closed canopy. The forests alternate with extensive patches of grasslands. Periyar's rich birdlife includes the Giant Hornbill, Cormorant, Darter, Osprey and Racket-tailed Drongo. The Indian Python and King Cobra are among the reptilian fauna. Periyar has a few Nilgiri Tahr, good numbers of which may also be seen on a day excursion to nearby Erivakulam National Park near Munnar.

Season: Open year-round, the best period being November-April.

Access: Fly to Cochin and drive to Periyar (200 km). The nearest railway station is Kottayam (114 km).

Accommodation and facilities: Near the lake within the park is a tourist complex run by Kerala Tourism, including Aranya Niwas, Periyar House and Lake Palace (further inside the park). The Spice Village is at the park entrance. Nearby is the new Garden Retreat (opening 1997). The park is best explored by boat. It is also possible to walk along selected trails in the park with a local guide.

Mammals:

Bonnet Macaque	Liontail Macaque	Nilgiri Langur
Golden Jackal	Bengal Fox	Dhole
Sloth Bear	Eurasian Otter	Smooth-coated Otter
Small Indian Civet	Common Palm Civet	Indian Grey Mongoose
Ruddy Mongoose	Stripe-necked Mongoose	Leopard Cat
Jungle Cat	Rusty-spotted Cat	Fishing Cat
Leopard	Tiger	Indian Elephant
Wild Boar	Indian Spotted Chevrotain	Indian Muntjac
Sambar	Gaur	Nilgiri Tahr
Indian Pangolin	Indian Palm Squirrel	Indian Giant Squirrel
Indian Porcupine	Indian Hare	

Indian Hare

110

PERIYAR NATIONAL PARK (INDIA)

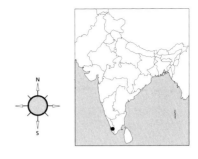

To Madurai ▲

Mangla Devi

Kumili Thekkadi

Madurai District

Spice Village
Taj Garden Retreat

Aranya Nivas

Pambanar

Kottayam
Forest Division

Azhutha River

Lake Palace

Vellimalai

Kottamalai

Sabarimala
Temple

Tamil Nadu

Pamba River

Moozhiyaar

To Kottayam, Cochin ◄

Ranni Forest
Division

Nagamalai

Manikmalai

Udamalai

Periyar River

Tottimalai

Pulamalai

Kalimalai

Town/Village/Place	●
Lodge/Hotel	⌂
Road/Track	
River	
Boundary	

111

17. RANTHAMBHOR NATIONAL PARK (INDIA)

Area: 39,200 hectares.
Established: 1955 as a sanctuary, 1973 as a tiger reserve, 1981 as a national park.
Description: Ranthambhor National Park is noted for its daylight sightings of the Tiger which appears to be more diurnal and less shy here than in most other parts of the subcontinent. The park lies in the Aravalli and the Vindhya range of hills and besides its importance as a haven for wildlife, is steeped in history. The park is dominated by the ruins of the 1,000 year-old Ranthambhor Fort within whose compounds roam Leopard and other denizens of the forest. Nearby are three lakes - Raj Bagh, Padam Talav and Malik Talav - where mammals congregate, especially during the dry months, when there is a shortage of water elsewhere. At that time of year the vegetation is not dense, which improves visibility and offers the best opportunities for mammal watching and photography. Tigers have been known to pursue Sambar that enter these lakes to drink and to wallow. Along the banks Marsh Crocodiles are occasionally seen sunning themselves during the winter. The forests are tropical dry deciduous, with trees of Ber, Babool, Katha, Jamun and Palash. Wolf is found in the adjoining Kaila Devi sanctuary.
Season: October-June, the best period being December-April.
Access: Drive from the nearest airport at Jaipur (132 km, 4 hours) or from the nearest railway station at Sawai Madhopur (14 km).
Accommodation and facilities: There are several lodges and camps outside the park, all within about 12 km of the park entrance. Sawai Madhopur Lodge is the former Maharaja of Jaipur's hunting lodge. Others include Tiger Moon, Castle Jhoomer Baori and Anurag Hotel. There are good motorable roads within the park and safaris are by 4-wheel drive motor vehicles and Canter mini vans. It is possible to walk up to the fort.

Mammals:

Hanuman Langur	Golden Jackal	Bengal Fox
Sloth Bear	Ratel	Small Indian Civet
Common Palm Civet	Small Indian Mongoose	Indian Grey Mongoose
Ruddy Mongoose	Striped Hyaena	Leopard Cat
Caracal	Jungle Cat	Wild Cat
Fishing Cat	Leopard	Tiger
Wild Boar	Chital	Sambar
Nilgai	Indian Gazelle	Northern Palm Squirrel
Indian Porcupine	Indian Hare	

Jungle Cat

112

RANTHAMBHOR NATIONAL PARK (INDIA)

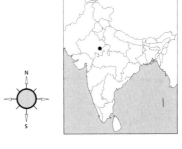

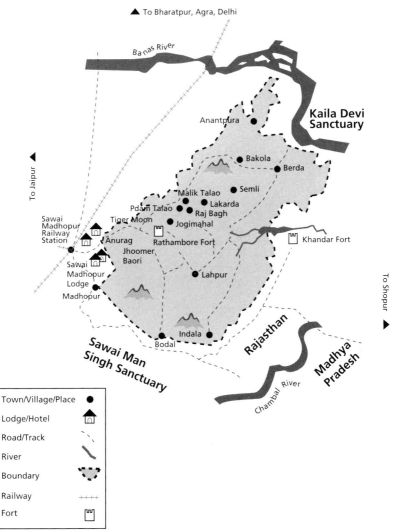

▲ To Bharatpur, Agra, Delhi

Banas River

Anantpura

Kaila Devi Sanctuary

Bakola

Berda

To Jaipur ▲

Semli

Malik Talao

Lakarda

Padam Talao

Raj Bagh

Tiger Moon

Jogimahal

Sawai
Madhopur
Railway
Station

Anurag

Rathambore Fort

Khandar Fort

Jhoomer
Baori

Sawai
Madhopur
Lodge

Lahpur

To Shopur ▲

Madhopur

Indala

Bodal

Sawai Man Singh Sanctuary

Rajasthan

Madhya Pradesh

Chambal River

Town/Village/Place	●
Lodge/Hotel	🏠
Road/Track	- - -
River	～
Boundary	▨
Railway	++++
Fort	⌂

113

18. SAGARMATHA OR MOUNT EVEREST NATIONAL PARK (NEPAL)

Area: 114,800 hectares. Adjoining it are 233,000 hectares of the Makalu-Barun national park and conservation area.

Established: 1976 as a national park.

Description: Among all the Himalayan national parks Sagarmatha has the distinction of being the highest, with Mount Sagarmatha (or Everest) at 8,848 metres. The park is entirely mountainous, the lowest point being at Jorsalle at 2,845 metres. Originating from the snow-clad high mountains in the east, north and west, are numerous glaciers that form the headwaters of the park's several rivers, notably the Dudh Kosi, Imja and Bhote Kosi. Sagarmatha is also the home of some 3,500 Sherpas who settled here from eastern Tibet during medieval times and have built several monasteries. In recent decades the Sherpas have earned a reputation as excellent mountain guides and climbers. A very small part of the park, along the lower river basin in the south, is forested, with trees such as Blue Pine, Fir, Birch, Juniper and Rhododendron. Nearly a third of the park is grazing land. Above 5,000 metres elevation the land is barren, with rocks, snow and ice. Sagarmatha is a good place to see Himalayan Tahr and Musk Deer. Birds include the Raven, Red-billed Chough, Golden Eagle, Lammergeier, Tibetan Snow-cock, and Impeyan and Blood Pheasants. The great attraction of Sagarmatha, however, is its spectacular natural beauty which draws thousands of trekkers each year from around the world. There is a visitor information centre at Namche Bazaar.

Season: Open year-round, the best periods being October-November and April-May.

Access: Fly from Kathmandu to Lukla (1 hour) outside the southern edge of the park and trek in. It is important to acclimatise well to the high altitude and precaution should be taken in case you experience any sign of high altitude sickness (characterised by lethargy, nausea, disorientation, insomnia, lack of appetite, etc).

Accommodation and facilities: There is a national park lodge at Tengboche and several lodges and tea houses along the trekking trails in villages, operated by local Sherpas. The accommodation in these lodges is generally basic but varies from lodge to lodge. The Everest View Hotel, situated near the Shyangboche airstrip, is the finest hotel in the park offering superb panoramic views of the Himalaya, including Everest. A large number of visitors stay in trekking tents. For productive mammal watching it is best to spend more time in or near forests and areas away from human disturbance. There are several excellent trekking routes within the park.

Mammals:

Rhesus Macaque	Hanuman Langur	Golden Jackal
Wolf	Asiatic Black Bear	Red Panda
Himalayan Weasel	Yellow-throated Marten	Masked Palm Civet
Snow Leopard	Forest Musk Deer	Indian Muntjac
Common Goral	Mainland Serow	Himalayan Tahr
Himalayan Marmot	Royle's Pika	

Golden Jackal

114

SAGARMATHA OR MOUNT EVEREST
NATIONAL PARK (NEPAL)

Town/Village/Place	●
Lodge/Hotel	
Road/Track	
River	
Boundary	
Airport/Airstrip	✈

115

19. SARISKA NATIONAL PARK (INDIA)

Area: 76,580 hectares, of which 27,380 hectares is the core area.

Established: 1958 as a sanctuary, 1979 as a tiger reserve, 1982 as a national park.

Description: Sariska National Park lies in the Aravalli hills and is the former hunting preserve of the Maharaja of Alwar. Sariska itself is a wide valley with two large plateaus and is dotted with places of historical and religious interest, including the ruins of the Kankwari Fort, the 10th century Neelkanth temples, the Buddha Hanuman Temple near Pandupol, the Bharthari Temple near the park office, and the hot and cold springs of Taalvriksh. The large Siliserh Lake is at the north-eastern corner. The forests are dry deciduous, with trees of Dhak, Acacia, Ber and Salar. The Tigers of Sariska are largely nocturnal and are not as easily seen as those of Ranthambhor. The park also has good populations of Nilgai, Sambar and Chital. In the evenings, Indian Porcupine, Striped Hyaena, Indian Palm Civet and even Leopard are sometimes seen. The forests are lush during and immediately following the monsoon, but during the dry months of February-May there is a shortage of water and in consequence mammals are attracted to water holes. At this time of year visibility is good because of the sparse foliage. Sariska is excellent for birdwatching and has an unusually large population of Indian Peafowl.

Season: Open year round, the best period being November-April, especially March-April.

Access: The nearest airport is at Jaipur (115 km, 3 hours) and the nearest railway station is at Alwar (36 km). The drive from Delhi takes 5-6 hours.

Accommodation and facilities: The grand Sariska Palace near the park office is a large sprawling complex, the main palace having been converted into a hotel. It was built by the Maharaja of Alwar as a hunting lodge. Nearby is Tiger's Den, a tourist bungalow run by the government. There are good roads within the park and some watch towers. Safaris are by 4-wheel drive motor vehicles.

Mammals:

Rhesus Macaque	Hanuman Langur	Golden Jackal
Bengal Fox	Ratel	Small Indian Civet
Common Palm Civet	Small Indian Mongoose	Indian Grey Mongoose
Striped Hyaena	Caracal	Leopard Cat
Jungle Cat	Leopard	Tiger
Wild Boar	Chital	Sambar
Nilgai	Four-horned Antelope	Northern Palm Squirrel
Indian Porcupine	Indian Hare	

Ratel

116

SARISKA NATIONAL PARK (INDIA)

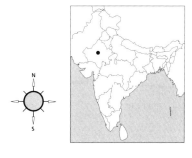

To Delhi

Alwar

Siliserh

Siliserh Lake

Taalvriksh

Raika

Baran

Thana Ghazi

Sariska Palace

Bharthari Temple

Park Office

Tiger's Den

Kankwari Fort

To Jaipur

Neelkanth

Kalighati

Pandupol

To Bharatpur, Agra

Raigarh

Khariwas

Tehla

Ajabgarh

Baswa

Gola Ka Bas

Bhangarh

Town/Village/Place	●
Lodge/Hotel	🏠
Road/Track	
River	
Boundary	
Fort	

20. SUKLA PHANTA WILDLIFE RESERVE (NEPAL)

Area: 15,500 hectares. Proposed extension by another 15,500 hectares.
Established: 1965 as a hunting reserve, 1976 as a wildlife reserve.
Description: Sukla Phanta is in the southwestern corner of Nepal, on the Indian border. The Mahakali river forms its western boundary and, together with the Chaughar river, drains the park. The park has a mixture of low hills up to 270 metres elevation and floodplains at 90 metres. On the uplands, which are not subject to prolonged waterlogging during the monsoons, grow the climax Sal forest. Along the rivers and the low-lying floodplains are found a rich mixture of grasslands and riverine forests, with Simal, Khair and Shisham trees. Large patches of grasslands are locally known as 'phantas' and harbour good numbers of the gregarious Swamp Deer. The park is named after the main 'phanta' called Sukla. There are a number of Marsh Crocodile and Python, and birds include Black-backed Woodpecker, Swamp Partridge and Common Crane.
Season: Open year round, the best period being November-April, especially March-April. Avoid the monsoons (June-October).
Access: Fly from Kathmandu to Mahendranagar and drive to the park. Alternatively drive to Sukla Phanta from Bardia via the bridge at Chisapani (4 hours). The park is also accessible by road from Corbett (6-7 hours) and Dudhwa (8-9 hours) in India.
Accommodation and facilities: There is a private tented camp, Silent Safari, inside the park. Safaris are by riding elephants, 4-wheel drive motor vehicles and on foot.

Mammals:

Rhesus Macaque	Hanuman Langur	Golden Jackal
Wolf	Bengal Fox	Dhole
Sloth Bear	Asiatic Black Bear	Eurasian Otter
Smooth Indian Otter	Small Indian Civet	Small Indian Mongoose
Indian Grey Mongoose	Striped Hyaena	Jungle Cat
Leopard	Tiger	Indian Elephant
Wild Boar	Indian Muntjac	Chital
Swamp Deer	Hog Deer	Sambar
Nilgai	Blackbuck	Indian Pangolin
Northern Palm Squirrel	Red Giant Flying Squirrel	Indian Porcupine
Hispid Hare	Indian Hare	

Indian Muntjac

SUKLA PHANTA WILDLIFE RESERVE (NEPAL)

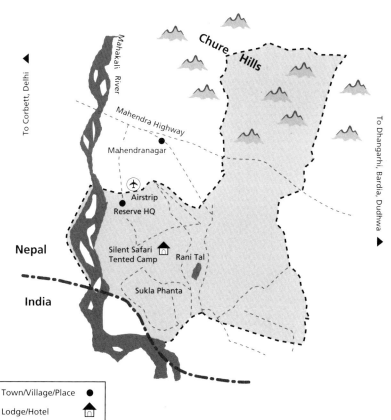

Town/Village/Place ●

Lodge/Hotel 🏠

Road/Track

River

Boundary

International Border

Airport/Airstrip ✈

21. SUNDERBANS NATIONAL PARK (INDIA) SUNDERBANS WILDLIFE SANCTUARIES (BANGLADESH)

Area: Sunderbans National Park, India, 169,950 hectares (core) and 88,527 hectares (buffer). Sunderbans West, Bangladesh, 9,069 hectares. Sunderbans South, Bangladesh 17,878 hectares. Sunderbans East, Bangladesh, 5,439 hectares.

Established: India, 1973 as a tiger reserve, 1978 as a national park. Bangladesh, 1977 as wildlife sanctuaries.

Description: Some believe that the name Sunderbans is derived from 'Sundri' - a plant found in the local mangroves - and 'bans' meaning forest. Others believe the name means 'beautiful forest' ('sunder' = beautiful, and 'bans' = forest). The Sunderbans, extending over an area of 1,000,000 hectares, is the world's largest delta, formed by the Ganges, Brahmaputra and Meghana rivers. The region has extensive mangrove forests and the contours are in a constant state of flux, caused by the monsoon flooding each year. Roughly a third of the delta is water, consisting of rivers, channels and tidal creeks up to 5 kilometres wide. The Sunderbans falls both within India and Bangladesh, the latter having the larger share of the delta. On the Indian side there is a national park overlooking the Bay of Bengal. The Sunderbans West, South and East wildlife sanctuaries in Bangladesh are also at the southern extremities of the delta. The Sunderbans parks are covered in mangrove forests of which there are 3 main zones, depending on the level of salt in the soil and water - a freshwater zone, a moderately saline zone, and a saline zone. Fishing, timber extraction and honey collection are the main human activities allowed within the Sunderbans. The four Sunderbans national parks have been lumped together as they all share common features of the estuarine mangrove ecosystem. The main attractions of the Sunderbans are the Tiger, of which the delta harbours the largest population in the world (some 300). The mangroves harbour large reptiles like the Monitor Lizard, Estuarine Crocodile and the Olive Ridley Turtle, for which there is a conservation programme

Fishing Cat

SUNDERBANS NATIONAL PARK (INDIA)

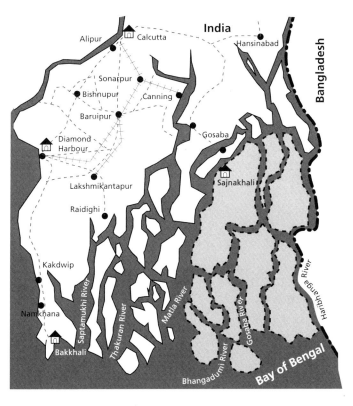

India

Alipur

Calcutta

Hansinabad

Bangladesh

Sonarpur

Bishnupur

Canning

Baruipur

Diamond
Harbour

Gosaba

Lakshmikantapur

Sajnakhali

Raidighi

Kakdwip

Saptamukhi River

Thakuran River

Matla River

Gosaba River

Bhangadumi River

Haribhanga River

Namkhana

Bakkhali

Bay of Bengal

Town/Village/Place	●
Lodge/Hotel	
Road/Track	
River	
Boundary	
Railway	++++

in the Indian park. The Leopard, Indian Rhinoceros, Javan Rhinoceros, Swamp Deer, Hog Deer and Water Buffalo have all become locally extinct from the delta in recent decades.

Season: November-April, the best period being December-February. Avoid during the monsoon (June-September).

Access: The Sunderbans are not easily accessible. To get to the Sunderbans national park in India the nearest airport is Calcutta, the nearest railway station is Canning, and the nearest town is Gosaba. From the park headquarters at Canning take the country motor launch (5 hours) to Sajnakhali. To get to the Sunderbans sanctuaries in Bangladesh, fly from Dacca to Jessore and drive to the port of Mongla (80 km) from where motor launches to Katka (8-9 hours) are available. Or from Jessore to the park headquarters at Khulna. This is a small port, so motor launches into the park are not generally available.

Accommodation and facilities: The Sunderbans lack the infrastructure for tourism and will only appeal to diehard mammal watchers. In the Bangladesh Sunderbans there is a Forest Department Guest House at Katka and the Port Authority Rest House at Nilkamal. In the Indian Sunderbans there is a basic Tourist Lodge at Sajnakhali run by Bengal Tourism. Transport within all the parks is by motor launch and boats as the entire mangroves are subject to daily inundation by the high tides from the sea.

Mammals:

Assam Macaque	Rhesus Macaque	Golden Jackal
Bengal Fox	Small Indian Civet	Indian Grey Mongoose
Smooth-coated Otter	Oriental Small-clawed Otter	Leopard Cat
Jungle Cat	Fishing Cat	Tiger
Ganges Dolphin	Wild Boar	Chital
Indian Muntjac	Indian Palm Squirrel	

Rhesus Macaque

SUNDERBANS WILDLIFE SANCTUARIES (BANGLADESH)

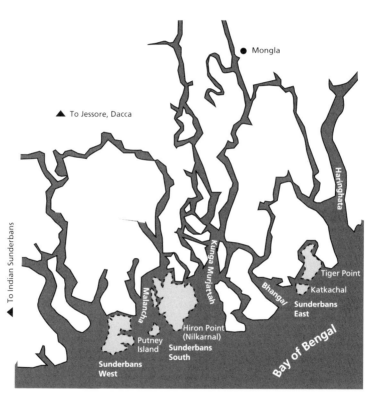

● Mongla

▲ To Jessore, Dacca

Haringhata

To Indian Sunderbans

▲ To Indian Sunderbans

Kunga Murjattah

Tiger Point

Bhangal

Katkachal

Sunderbans East

Malancha

Hiron Point (Nilkarnal)

Putney Island

Sunderbans South

Sunderbans West

Bay of Bengal

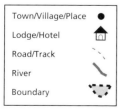

Town/Village/Place ●

Lodge/Hotel

Road/Track

River

Boundary

123

22. WILPATTU NATIONAL PARK (SRI LANKA)

Area: 131,693 hectares.

Established: 1938 as a national park.

Description: The picturesque Wilpattu National Park lies 175 km due north of Colombo within the districts of Puttalam and Anuradhapura on the north-western coast of Sri Lanka and overlooks the Indian Ocean. The western coastal parts of the park are covered in extremely fine copper red sand. Wilpattu has numerous 'villus' or lakes which are excellent places for mammal watching. The 'villus' are not natural lakes, but depressions in the soil that annually accumulate rain water and are found throughout Sri Lanka. Two of them, Kokkari and Luniwila, are as saline as the sea. The park is covered in a mixture of secondary tropical forests, mainly dense, alternating with open sandy areas. Along the western parts there are thorny scrub forests, reminiscent of Yala National Park to the south. Wilpattu is also one of the best places in the subcontinent to see Leopard - they are the dominant predator (unlike in India where they are subordinate to the Tiger) and may be seen in broad daylight. Sloth Bear is also regularly seen, especially when the Palu and Veera plants are in fruit in May-June. The park also has a good population of the Indian Elephant, Indian Muntjac and Indian Spotted Chevrotain.

Season: Open year round, the best periods being February-March and May-September.

Access: Wilpattu is easily accessible from Colombo or Anuradhapura by road.

Accommodation and facilities: There are a number of lodges in the park overlooking the 'villus' and one overlooking a river. There is also accommodation outside the park. The park has a network of 240 km of roads and is best explored by 4-wheel-drive vehicles.

Mammals:

Hanuman Langur	Sloth Bear	Eurasian Otter
Small Indian Civet	Common Palm Civet	Indian Grey Mongoose
Ruddy Mongoose	Stripe-necked Mongoose	Jungle Cat
Rusty-spotted Cat	Leopard	Indian Elephant
Wild Boar	Indian Spotted Chevrotain	Indian Muntjac
Chital	Hog Deer	Sambar
Water Buffalo	Indian Pangolin	Indian Palm Squirrel
Grizzled Indian Squirrel	Indian Porcupine	Indian Hare

Wild Boar

WILPATTU NATIONAL PARK (SRI LANKA)

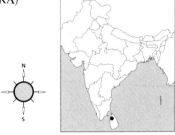

Kondaichchi

Periyamurippo

Portugal
Bay

Marichchukkaddi

Kudermalai
Point

Tantirilmalai

To Anuradhapura ▶

Kokmotte

Kali Villu

Kokkare Villu

Tala Wila

Maradanmaduwa

Pomparippu

Hunuwilagama

Illavankulam

Katupatwew

Hotel Wilpattu

Timbirlwewa

Wildlife Protection
Society Lodge

Kalu Oya River

Puliyankulama

Periganagavillu

▼ To Puttalam, Colombo

Town/Village/Place	●
Lodge/Hotel	
Road/Track	
River	
Boundary	

125

23. YALA WEST OR RUHUNA NATIONAL PARK (SRI LANKA)

Area: Yala West (Block 1) 13,679 hectares.
Established: 1938 as a national park.
Description: Yala lies on the south-eastern corner of Sri Lanka, some 350 km from Colombo. The open scrub forests of Yala and its grassy plains are reminiscent of the African bush and because of the better visibility are an excellent place for mammal watching. The grasslands are dotted with waterholes where mammals come to drink and bathe, and outcrops of huge boulders often used as hideouts by animals, the larger ones occasionally with their own 'kemas' or pools of water. The star attraction of Yala is the Indian Elephant, 10-30 of whom may often be seen together, especially after the rains during January-May, when the regrowth of new succulent grasses and plants is abundant. Unlike in India, however, the males are usually tuskless, large tuskers being extremely rare. The park also has a good number of Leopard. The Sloth Bear is another attraction of Yala best seen in late May and June when the Veera and Palu plants (to which the animal is very partial) are in fruit. On a good day 2-3 of these shaggy creatures may be seen. The park contains the ruins of ancient temples and monasteries and also harbours the Estuarine Crocodile and over 200 species of birds.
Season: Open year round, the best time being November-July.
Access: Drive to the park entrance at Palatupana from Colombo via Galle on the southern coast, or via Ratnapura in the interior.
Accommodation and facilities: There are several lodges within the park and a few outside. Inside the park there are some 50 km of good roads and a further 40 km of dirt tracks that can be used with 4-wheel drive vehicles. Within a few hours' drive from Yala/Ruhuna are some very good hotels and resorts along the southern coasts of Sri Lanka.

Mammals:

Hanuman Langur	Golden Jackal	Sloth Bear
Eurasian Otter	Small Indian Civet	Common Palm Civet
Indian Grey Mongoose	Ruddy Mongoose	Stripe-necked Mongoose
Rusty-spotted Cat	Leopard	Indian Elephant
Wild Boar	Indian Spotted Chevrotain	Indian Muntjac
Chital	Sambar	Water Buffalo
Indian Pangolin	Indian Palm Squirrel	Grizzled Indian Squirrel
Indian Porcupine	Indian Hare	

Sloth Bear

126

YALA WEST OR RUHUNA NATIONAL PARK (SRI LANKA)

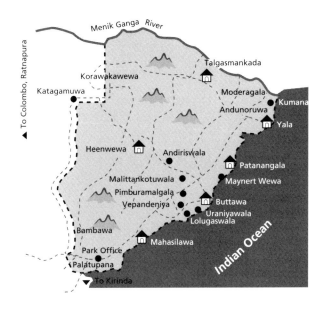

Town/Village/Place	●
Lodge/Hotel	
Road/Track	
River	
Boundary	

CHECKLIST OF THE MAMMALS OF THE INDIAN SUBCONTINENT
(included in this book)

☐ Asiatic Black Bear (Selenarctos thibetanus)
☐ Asiatic Golden Cat (Felis temminckii)
☐ Asiatic Wild Ass (Equus hemionus)
☐ Assam Macaque (Macaca assamensis)

☐ Beech Marten (Martes foina)
☐ Bengal Fox (Vulpes bengalensis)
☐ Bharal (Pseudois nayaur)
☐ Binturong (Arctictis binturong)
☐ Black Giant Squirrel (Ratufa bicolor)
☑ Blackbuck (Antilope cervicapra)
☐ Bonnet Macaque (Macaca radiata)
☐ Brown Bear (Ursus arctos)

☐ Capped Leaf Monkey (Presbytis pileatus)
☐ Caracal (Felis caracal)
☐ Chiru (Pantholops hodgsonii)
☐ Chital (Cervus axis)
☐ Clouded Leopard (Neofelis nebulosa)
☐ Common Goral (Nemorhaedus goral)
☐ Common Palm Civet (Paradoxurus hermaphroditus)
☐ Crab-eating Mongoose (Herpestes vitticollis)

☐ Dhole (Cuon alpinus)

☐ Eurasian Lynx (Lynx lynx)
☐ Eurasian Otter (Lutra lutra)

☐ Fishing Cat (Felis viverrina)
☐ Forest Musk Deer (Moschus chrysogaster)
☐ Four-horned Antelope (Tetracerus quadricornis)

☐ Ganges Dolphin (Platanista gangetica)
☐ Gaur (Bos gaurus)
☐ Golden Jackal (Canis aureus)
☐ Golden Leaf Monkey (Presbytis geei)
☐ Grizzled Indian Squirrel (Ratufa macroura)

☐ Hanuman Langur (Presbytis entellus)
☐ Himalayan Marmot (Marmota himalayana)
☐ Himalayan Tahr (Hemitragus jemlahicus)
☐ Himalayan Weasel (Mustela sibirica)
☐ Hispid Hare (Caprolagus hispidus)

☐ Hodgson's Short-tailed Porcupine (Hystrix brachyura/hodgsonii)
☐ Hog Deer (Cervus porcinus)
☐ Hoolock Gibbon (Hylobates hoolock)

☐ Ibex (Capra ibex)
☐ Indian Elephant (Elephas maximus)
☐ Indian Gazelle (Gazella bennettii)
☐ Indian Giant Squirrel (Ratufa indica)
☑ Indian Grey Mongoose (Herpestes edwardsii)
☐ Indian Hare (Lepus nigricollis)
☐ Indian Muntjac (Muntiacus muntjac)
☐ Indian Palm Squirrel (Funambulus palmarum)
☐ Indian Pangolin (Manis crassicaudata)
☐ Indian Porcupine (Hystrix indica)
☐ Indian Rhinoceros (Rhinoceros unicornis)
☐ Indian Spotted Chevrotain (Tragulus meminna)

☐ Jungle Cat (Felis chaus)

☐ Kashmir Pygmy Flying Squirrel (Hylopetes fimbriatus)

☐ Large-eared Pika (Ochotona macrotis)
☐ Large Indian Civet (Viverra zibetha)
☐ Leopard (Panthera pardus)
☐ Leopard Cat (Felis bengalensis)
☐ Lion (Panthera leo)
☑ Liontail Macaque (Macaca silenus)
☐ Long-tailed Marmot (Marmota caudata)

☐ Mainland Serow (Capricornis sumatraensis)
☐ Marbled Cat (Felis marmorata)
☐ Markhor (Capra falconeri)
☐ Masked Palm Civet (Paguma larvata)
☐ Mountain Weasel (Mustela altaica)

☐ Nilgai (Boselaphus tragocamelus)
☐ Nilgiri Langur (Presbytis johnii)
☐ Nilgiri Tahr (Hemitragus hylocrius)
☐ Northern Palm Squirrel (Funambulus pennantii)

☐ Orange-bellied Himalayan Squirrel (Dremomys lokriah)
☐ Oriental Small-clawed Otter (Aonyx cinerea)

☐ Pallas's Cat (Felis manul)
☐ Particoloured Flying Squirrel (Hylopetes alboniger)
☐ Pygmy Hog (Sus salvanius)

☐ Ratel (Mellivora capensis)
☐ Red Deer (Cervus elaphus)
☐ Red Fox (Vulpes vulpes)

☐ Red Giant Flying Squirrel (Petaurista petaurista)
☐ Red Panda (Ailurus fulgens)
☐ Rhesus Macaque (Macaca mulatta)
☐ Royle's Pika (Ochotona roylei)
☐ Ruddy Mongoose (Herpestes smithii)
☐ Rusty-spotted Cat (Felis rubiginosa)

☐ Sambar (Cervus unicolor)
☐ Sloth Bear (Melursus ursinus)
☐ Slow Loris (Nycticebus coucang)
☐ Small Indian Civet (Viverricula indica)
☐ Small Indian Mongoose (Herpestes auropunctatus)
☐ Smooth-coated Otter (Lutra perspicillata)
☐ Snow Leopard (Panthera uncia)
☐ Spotted Linsang (Prionodon pardicolor)
☐ Striped Hyaena (Hyaena hyaena)
☐ Stripe-necked Mongoose (Herpestes vitticollis)
☐ Swamp Deer (Cervus duvauceli)

☐ Takin (Budorcas taxicolor)
☐ Thamin (Cervus eldii)
☐ Three-striped Palm Civet (Arctogalidea trivirgata)
☐ Tiger (Panthera tigris)

☐ Water Buffalo (Bubalus arnee)
☐ Wild Boar (Sus scrofa)
☐ Wild Cat (Felis silvestris)
☐ Wild Goat (Capra aegagrus)
☐ Wolf (Canis lupus)

☐ Yak (Bos mutus)
☐ Yellow-bellied Weasel (Mustela kathiah)
☐ Yellow-throated Marten (Martes flavigula)

FURTHER READING

Ahmad M F and S A Ghalib, A CHECKLIST OF MAMMALS OF PAKISTAN, *in Records Zoological Survey of Pakistan, Vol VII Nos 1 and 2, pages 1-34, Karachi, January and July 1975*

Alderton D and B Tanner, WILD CATS OF THE WORLD, *Blandford, London, 1993*

Bedi R, CORBETT NATIONAL PARK, *Clarion Books, Delhi, 1984*

Bhatt D D and T K Shreshtha, THE ENVIRONMENT OF SUKLA PHANTA, *Tribhuvan University Press, Kathmandu, 1977*

Bunting B W and R M Wright, ANNAPURNA NATIONAL PARK: THE NEPAL PLAN FOR JOINING HUMAN VALUES AND CONSERVATION OF A MOUNTAIN ECOSYSTEM, in People and Protected Areas in the Hindu Kush-Himalaya, *KMTNC and ICIMOD, Kathmandu, 1985*

Catton C, PANDAS, *Christopher Helm, London, 1990*

Chapman J and J Flux (Editors), RABBITS, HARES AND PIKAS, STATUS SURVEY AND CONSERVATION ACTION PLAN, IUCN, *Gland, 1990*

Chatterjee A K and S S Chandiramani, AN INTRODUCTION TO NAMDAPHA TIGER RESERVE, ARUNACHAL PRADESH, INDIA, *Tiger Paper, 13 (3), 1986*

Corbet G B and J E Hill, A WORLD LIST OF MAMMALIAN SPECIES, *2nd Ed, Facts on File Publications, New York, & British Museum (Natural History), London, 1986*

Corbet G B and J E Hill, THE MAMMALS OF THE INDOMALAYAN REGION, *Natural History Museum Publications, London/Oxford University Press, Oxford, 1992*

Director, Zoological Survey of India (Editor), THE RED DATA BOOK OF INDIAN ANIMALS, PART 1: VERTEBRATA, *Zoological Survey of India, Calcutta, 1994*

Earl of Cranbrook, MAMMALS OF SOUTHEAST ASIA, 2nd Edition, *Oxford University Press, Singapore, 1991*

Ellerman J R and T C S Morrison-Scott, CHECKLIST OF PALAEARCTIC AND INDIAN MAMMALS 1758-1946, *British Museum, London, 1951*

Foster-Turley et al (Editors), OTTERS, AN ACTION PLAN FOR THEIR CONSERVATION, IUCN, *Gland, 1990*

Ganhar J N, THE WILDLIFE OF LADAKH, Haramukh Publications, *Srinagar, 1979*

Gee E P, THE WILD LIFE OF INDIA, *Collins, London, 1964*

Green M J B (Editor), NATURE RESERVES OF THE HIMALAYA AND THE

MOUNTAINS OF CENTRAL ASIA, *Oxford University Press, New Delhi, 1993*

Gurung K K, HEART OF THE JUNGLE, *Andre Deutsch, London, 1983*

Inskipp C, A POPULAR GUIDE TO THE BIRDS AND MAMMALS OF THE ANNAPURNA CONSERVATION AREA, ACAP/KMTNC, *Kathmandu, 1989*

Israel S, et al (Editors), INDIAN WILDLIFE, *APA Publications, Singapore, 1992*

Jayewardene H W (Editor), YALA NATIONAL PARK, *Fauna International Trust, Colombo, 1993*

Jefferies M, MOUNT EVEREST NATIONAL PARK, *The Mountaineers, Seattle, 1991*

Jerdon T C, THE MAMMALS OF INDIA, *Reprint, Mittal Publications, Delhi, 1984*

Khan M A R, MAMMALS OF BANGLADESH, *Nazima Reza, Dhaka, 1985*

Kitchener A, THE NATURAL HISTORY OF THE WILD CATS, *Christopher Helm, London, 1991*

Krishnan M, INDIA'S WILDLIFE IN 1959-1970, *Bombay Natural History Society, Bombay, 1975*

Krishnan M, THE HANDBOOK OF INDIA'S WILDLIFE, *Maps and Agencies, Madras, 1983*

Laidler, K and L Laidler, PANDAS: GIANTS OF THE BAMBOO FOREST, *BBC Books, London, 1992*

Lekagul B and J McNeely, MAMMALS OF THAILAND, *2nd Edition, Association for the Conservation of Wildlife, Bangkok, 1988*

Macdonald D (Editor), THE ENCYCLOPEDIA OF MAMMALS, *Fact on File, New York, 1993*

Mishra H R and M Jefferies, ROYAL CHITWAN NATIONAL PARK: WILDLIFE HERITAGE OF NEPAL, *The Mountaineers, Seattle, 1991*

Mishra H and D Mierow, WILD ANIMALS OF NEPAL, *Kathmandu, 1976*

Napier J R and P H Napier, THE NATURAL HISTORY OF THE PRIMATES, *British Museum (Natural History), London, 1985*

Nowak R M, WALKERS MAMMALS OF THE WORLD, *5th Edition, Volumes 1 and 2, The John Hopkins University Press, Baltimore and London, 1991*

Nowell K and P Jackson (Editors), WILD CATS, STATUS SURVEY AND CONSERVATION ACTION PLAN, IUCN, *Gland, 1996*

Oliver W L R, THE PIGMY HOG, *Jersey Wildlife Preservation Trust, Jersey, 1980*

Oliver W L R, THE DISTRIBUTION AND STATUS OF THE HISPID HARE, *Jersey Wildlife Preservation Trust, Jersey, 1985*

Parker S P (Editor), GRZIMEK'S ENCYCLOPEDIA OF MAMMALS, Volumes 1-5, *McGraw Hill, London, 1990*

Phillips W W A, MANUAL OF THE MAMMALS OF SRI LANKA, Parts 1-3, 2nd Edition, *Wildlife and Nature Protection Society of Sri Lanka, Colombo, 1980-1984*

Prater S H, THE BOOK OF INDIAN ANIMALS, 3rd Edition, *Bombay Natural History Society, Bombay, 1980*

Roberts T J, THE MAMMALS OF PAKISTAN, *Ernest Benn, London, 1977*

Saharia V B (Editor), WILDLIFE IN INDIA, *Department of Agriculture and Cooperation, New Delhi, 1981*

Schaller G B, THE DEER AND THE TIGER, *Chicago University Press, Chicago, 1967*

Scientific Exploration Society, THE NAMDAPHA RAINFOREST PROJECT - JANUARY 1994, *unpublished manuscript, Dorset, 1994*

Scott D A (Editor), A DIRECTORY OF ASIAN WETLANDS, IUCN, *Gland and Cambridge, 1989*

Sharma B D, HIGH ALTITUDE WILDLIFE OF INDIA, *Oxford and IBH Publishing, New Delhi, 1994*

Singh R (Editor), BIRD AND WILD LIFE SANCTUARIES OF INDIA, NEPAL AND BHUTAN, *Nest and Wings, New Delhi, 1980*

Smythies E A, BIG GAME SHOOTING IN NEPAL, *Thaker Spink and Co, Calcutta, 1942*

Stirling I (Editor), BEARS, MAJESTIC CREATURES OF THE WILD, *HarperCollins, London, 1993*

Tikader B K, THREATENED ANIMALS OF INDIA, *Zoological Society of India, Calcutta, 1983*

Tyabji H, BANDHAVGARH NATIONAL PARK: A GUIDE, *New Delhi, 1994*

Upreti B N, ROYAL BARDIA NATIONAL PARK, *NPC/IUCN National Conservation Strategy Implementation Project, Kathmandu, 1994*

Ward P and S Kynaston, BEARS OF THE WORLD, *Blandford, London, 1995*

WCMC and IUCN/CNPPA, 1993 UN LIST OF NATIONAL PARKS AND PROTECTED AREAS, *IUCN, Gland, 1994*

133

INDEX OF MAMMALS (Common Names)

134

Goral, Common, 40
Hare, Hispid, 49
Hare, Indian, 49
Hog, Pygmy, 32
Hyaena, Striped, 24

Ibex, 42

Jackal, Golden, 14

Langur, Hanuman, 12
Langur, Nilgiri, 13
Leopard, 29
Leopard, Clouded, 30
Leopard, Snow, 30
Linsang, Spotted, 21
Lion, 28
Loris, Slow, 10
Lynx, Eurasian, 28

Macaque, Assam, 10
Macaque, Bonnet, 11
Macaque, Liontail, 11
Macaque, Rhesus, 10
Markhor, 42
Marmot, Himalayan, 46
Marmot, Long-tailed, 46
Marten, Beech, 19
Marten, Yellow-throated, 18
Mongoose, Crab-eating, 24
Mongoose, Indian Grey, 23
Mongoose, Ruddy, 24

INDEX OF MAMMALS (Scientific Names)

Ailurus fulgens, 17
Antilope cervicapra, 39
Aonyx cinerea, 20
Arctictis binturong, 23
Arctogalidea trivirgata, 22

Bos gaurus, 38
Bos mutus, 38
Boselaphus tragocamelus, 36
Bubalus arnee, 38
Budorcas taxicolor, 40

Canis aureus, 14
Canis lupus, 14
Capra aegagrus, 41
Capra falconeri, 42
Capra ibex, 42
Capricornis sumatraensis, 40
Caprolagus hispidus, 49
Cervus axis, 34
Cervus duvauceli, 35
Cervus elaphus, 35
Cervus eldii, 35
Cervus porcinus, 36
Cervus unicolor, 36
Cuon alpinus, 15

Dremomys lokriah, 45

Elaphus maximus, 31
Equus hemionus, 31

Felis bengalensis, 25
Felis caracal, 25
Felis chaus, 26
Felis manul, 26
Felis marmorata, 26
Felis rubiginosa, 27
Felis silvestris, 27
Felis temminckii, 27
Felis viverrina, 28
Funambulus palmarum, 43
Funambulus pennantii, 44

Gazella bennettii, 39

INDEX OF NATIONAL PARKS